CIVILIZED RELIGION

CIVILIZED RELIGION

An Historical and Philosophical Analysis

Herbert Wallace Schneider

AN EXPOSITION-UNIVERSITY BOOK

Exposition Press   *New York*

EXPOSITION PRESS INC.

50 Jericho Turnpike   Jericho, New York 11753

FIRST EDITION

LIBRARY OF CONGRESS CATALOG CARD NUMBER: 79-186484

0-682-47426-6

Contents

Preface   7

I   DEVOTION   11
    The Devoted Self   11
    Self-Conscious Devotion   12
    Interpersonal Devotion or Love   13
II   RELIGIOUS DEVOTION   15
III   HOLY ORDERS AND SACRED SCRIPTURES   18
    Holy Men and Women   18
    Monasticism   20
    Other Religious Orders   22
    Sacred Scriptures   24
    Devotional Writings   30
IV   SANCTUARIES, SHRINES AND TEMPLES   32
    Places of Refuge   32
    Tombs   33
    Residences for Ancestral Spirits   34
    Shrines   35
    Altars   35
    Temples   37
V   RELIGIOUS EXPRESSIONS AND SYMBOLS   38
    The Language and Posture of Prayer   38
    Confession   41
    Purification Rites   41
    Praise   43
VI   COMMUNION AND PUBLIC WORSHIP   45
    Congregation   45
    Mysteries   47
    Covenants   47

	Synagogues	48
	Mosques and Sufis	49
	Types of Christian Communion	50
	Communions and World Community	52
VII	SACRA, SACRAMENTS, AND THE SACRED	54
	A Celebration of Buddha's Birth	55
	An Early Christian Rite of Initiation Into the Mystery	56
	The Roman Creeds	59
	The East-West Schism in Christendom	61
	The Sacred	61
VIII	HOLY DAYS AND SEASONS	64
IX	RELIGIOUS BODIES AND SOCIAL SERVICES	70
	Institutional Religion	70
	Administration	71
	The Laity	72
	The Social Gospel	73
	Public Piety and Religious Movements	76
X	DIVINE BEINGS	78
	The Divine	78
	Heaven and Earth	79
	Pantheons	80
	Trinities	82
XI	MONOTHEISM AND HUMANISM	83
	The Cosmos	84
	Our God Is One Lord	85
	Humanistic Devotion	87
XII	FAITH AND FIDELITY	90
	Creeds and Faiths	92
	The Plurality of Faiths	93
	Types of Religious Experience	96
XIII	TWO COMMANDMENTS	99
XIV	THREE WISE MEN	104

Preface

RELIGION is more ancient than civilization, and religious institutions have had a long and bitter experience of what it means to be civilized. There is still a thriving abundance of uncivilized religion even within civilization, where it is a cultural liability and a disgrace to great traditions and to inspired revelations. But there is also conspicuous evidence of improvements, reforms, and revisions among religions, indicating that religious institutions are still learning the arts of civilization and that they are occasionally taking a leading part, as they often have done, in such arts. The current notion that religion is disappearing and that civilization will be promoted by this disappearance is certainly an illusion and wishful thinking on the part of those who are either ignorant of the power of religion or who have suffered under uncivilized uses of this power. Religion has deep roots in almost all cultures, and its vitality is never more in evidence than when it is being attacked. Religions are still coming into being and passing away, along with the cultures in which they are rooted. But they are not as fragile as are the theological superstructures and rationalizing fashions which pretend to protect or explain religious devotion. These intellectual systems, like the religions from which they spring, may or may not be well informed about civilization, and they may or may not be an asset to religious life. Whatever may happen to theology as a science, the arts of religion have greater vitality. However, the task of exercising a leading part in civilized life is more demanding and difficult than ever. No one knows this better than the clergy.

Though they are relatively durable, religions reflect the experience of generation after generation, as each learns to pass judgment on them. Beneath the slow transience of particular faiths, cults, and myths, there is a continual emergence of authentic, fresh religious life. There were poets before the art of poetry was known, and poets still prefer to read each others' poems rather than study the writings of professional critics. So also in religious life, men have been and still are religious before they have an understanding of a particular creed. They learn by hard experience, both bitter and ecumenical, how to become more civilized. Theologians, from time to time, try to help them by "de-mythologizing" their faiths, but such attempts are usually not the end of a faith but the beginning of a new mythology. Nietzsche is the classic example. Whatever the "higher" critics may say to the contrary, devout persons are apt to interpret faith and myth in terms of fidelity.

To tell the story of how religions have become civilized in history and experience would be a daring venture, for it would inevitably be corrupted by perspectives and prejudices. No such attempt is made here. Suffice it to identify some examples and aspects of authentic religious devotion in several religions and in several degrees of civilization. The illustrations and descriptions to which I resort may be ill chosen for others and unconvincing, but each reader will at least have the opportunity to judge for himself. All justice is difficult, to be sure, but in religion as in art, different religions, like individual artists, learn gradually to respect each other in their differences and to discover eventually how their own devotions may be civilized.

Claremont, California   H. W. S.
1971

CIVILIZED RELIGION

I. Devotion

The Devoted Self

THE religious life is a devoted life, but not all devotion is religious. Before examining what religion does to human devotion in general, and how devoutness is related to devotedness, we should be aware of how human beings become devoted to anything.

Many animals are very busy, and from a human point of view appear to be devoted workers. Ants, bees, and beavers are proverbial models of industry. What makes them appear to be genuine workers is that their busyness is centered in obvious usefulness; they seem to know what they need and how to get it. But it is easy to prove that they do not know why they are busy; to follow a definite way of life is simply their "nature." A distant observer, like the proverbial man in Mars, would probably regard human animals as just naturally busy. They need to be industrious to make a living. But even when at play human beings are apt to play intensively and competitively, concentrating their energies on acquiring skills with which they are not equipped by nature. It comes naturally to human beings to be intensely active, but the variety of their activities and objectives leads them in many directions and often to distraction. Human life involves facing obstacles and solving problems. Whether human beings are tempted into this way of life, as the myth of Adam and Eve suggests, or whether they are by nature forced into a struggle for existence, is a question for which there is no simple answer. Whatever the cause or origin, the fact is that human business is not mere instinct. Mankind is in circumstances which require concentration of energies and discipline. Even when a human animal seems to be spontaneously busy and merely emotionally devoted to its work or play, it really becomes involved in planning intelligently, in organizing its occupations, and in making order out of its activities. A wholehearted devotion to a few interests involves establishing priorities, making selections, and clarifying objectives. In short, a human being becomes serious.

An animal that can do this shows that it has a mind and that "minding its business" is different from just being busy. An ability to work on this basis is what gives the human animal preeminence. Such beings are known as persons or characters. Conscious and persistent devotion to a way of life, taking life seriously, is a sign of a healthy mind; it is the basis of the normal growth of an intelligent person. The objects of devotion may vary widely and are subject to change, but normally they gradually become organized, some of them becoming dominant. The quality and stability of devotion are the measures of a sense of values and of character. A person is known by the objects to which he gives himself and the ways in which he gives himself to them. Normally a life of devotion requires integration of interests and balancing of a variety of values and obligations. On the other hand, devotion may become morbid and obsessive; or a conflict of devotions may lead to frustration and disintegration. Devotions for better or for worse are in general neither good nor bad. They may make or break a person. Devotions are central to the self, but the self is not their object. Devotion is not self-love, as it has often been interpreted; it is usually extraverted. But even when it is introverted it usually does not have the self as its object; it has particular worries, anxieties, or obsessions.

Self-Conscious Devotion

As the increasing number and power of objects of devotion make their impact on the growing self, problems of self-control become urgent. Usually a few priorities become increasingly demanding and engrossing. Some of them become the enduring pattern of a career. In this process of self-formation there are apt to be crises, when devotion itself becomes a problem. Self-consciousness becomes acute; introversion may threaten integration. An anxious, self-conscious devotion and loss of objective focus is a natural stage in the approach to maturity. A critical inventory of interests becomes necessary, and decisions must be made that are serious, perhaps determining one's life. To whom and to what a person then decides to give himself becomes the most urgent practical problem. Devotion has then ceased to be a spontaneous emotional urge and has become a deliberately accepted way of life. Such a conscious giving or grounding of the self on some object or objective is usually not interpreted as self-sacrifice, but as self-fulfillment, or commitment. The aim of such an act is not to lose oneself, but to preserve and direct the self.

A radical expansion of intellectual interests, and an increasing obligation to the work one is devoted to, creates a complication, perhaps a conflict, that has serious consequences. When new areas are opened up for intellectual exploration at the same time that increased opportunities for participation in institutional activities arise, the result is not only excitement and stimulation, but also bewilderment. Thus the normal process of facing the complexities of maturity and community creates crises of devotion, and out of these crises come the basic decisions that determine the course which devotion will take, or the fate which devotion will endure.

Interpersonal Devotion or Love

When devotion is concerned not with external matters but with the relations among human beings, either individually or in groups, it assumes its greatest moral significance. Reciprocal devotion is the crown of love and close to the heart of happiness. But love and devotion have independent roots and origins in human nature and experience. They are not inseparable; each may go its own way. Together, they enhance each other, and their union makes a major contribution to the good life. But the great importance of love makes the problem of relating it to other forms of devotion one of the major concerns of any self.

To this problem there is no general solution. But it states one of the most general themes that we shall meet as we face religious devotion. The moral ties of interpersonal relations must be examined in their relation to the demands of work, art, science, play and the other objects of devotion.

The chief point of making these observations about the commonplaces of human life is to emphasize the complications which modern living creates for a life of devotion.

II. Religious Devotion

A religion takes devotion out of its practical context in human life and personal growth and gives it intrinsic forms, articulation, generalization, and celebration. Religious devotions cannot have much serious significance for a person who is not involved in the intricacies of practical devotion in daily life. If devotion is not a reality in secular life, devoutness must appear as artificial pretense at best and as an arbitrary burden at worst. Devotion is not created by religion; religion is created and nourished by devotion. Religion, when it is performing its proper service, enhances, clarifies, and strengthens daily devotions. Religion is not devotion to devotion, devotion for devotion's sake. And it is certainly not a devotion to religion. It is reasonable if it can make practical devotion more significant and more bearable. If it tries to undermine or make unbearable these devotions, it is worse than useless.

Our description of religion must therefore focus on the various ways in which the religions interpret the devotions in life, and on how these interpretations succeed or fail in promoting such devotions. Because of their peculiar power, religious devotions can be a blessing or a curse; they may be the finest expression of a healthy devoted life, or the worst form of fanaticism and a perversion of what should be serious into something trivial or deluded.

Religious devotions, like devotion in general, have a double function in human experience, commonly called "piety" and "ideality." Piety aims at making men aware of what is necessary or basic for human existence; ideality aims at making men aware of values and the good life. Piety takes seriously the natural conditions and resources of civilized life; ideality takes seriously the aims and perfections of human achievements. To use familiar metaphors, piety looks back and down; ideality looks forward and up. Piety keeps us aware of our heritage and resources, ideality urges us to pursue the good life. Though they appear to lead in opposite directions, they are complementary; they express the two dimensions of practical devotion. When either is cultivated without the other, the result is pathetic if not tragic. Piety without aim is blind; ideals without means are futile. Traditionalism and perfectionism have been the ruin of many a faith and of morale, both leading to frustration and delusion. Therefore, one of the major problems of religion as well as of morals and prudence is the art of making these two polar opposites promote each other. One of the basic ways in which religion can clarify the relations among the many devotions is its ability to keep a healthy balance between piety and ideality. Each alone, is in danger of fanaticism.

The formalized and generalized devotions of religious language, faith, and ceremonies must find their concrete meanings or content in the varied human devotions as they actually exist. Otherwise religion is empty formality. Formalities have a valuable place in all arts and sciences provided they actually formalize something that is not mere form to begin with. Being devout without being devoted brings religious observances into ill repute and hypocrisy. Formalities should not breed formalism; they are intended to serve those serious aspects of life that should not be left informal and vague or misguided and inadequately expressed. Religious observance is human service when it makes explicit much that would otherwise be felt but not recognized. Even platitudes and proverbs have their religious uses, but they are too much abused by being paraded as poetic insights and wisdom. The enormous amount of so-called "wisdom literature," of which religions have more than their share, becomes a redundant insistence on generalities more suitable for refrains in anthems than for "the beginning of wisdom." Similarly, the devotions of the devout are easily overdone, and they become positively harmful when they are regarded as mere obligations for holy days rather than useful as reflection on life in general.

The general critique of religions as an art of expression and clarification is complicated by a circumstance that is very personal. In estimating the values of devoutness it makes a great difference whether the observances in question are familiar in reference to secular experience. In all cultures religious observances are more or less standardized. Being an intrinsic aspect of a culture, religious rites and symbols have an entirely different meaning and function to one who finds them expressive from the way they are experienced by those who find them merely formal.

This complication is evident when a person familiar with only one religion tends to give vent to his rebellious emotions against that religion by attributing the faults of the repudiated forms to religion in general, or by adopting a religion that is extremely different from the one with which he was familiar. Thomas Hobbes defined superstition as "the other man's religion." It is too easy to condemn as superstition whatever myths, rites, sacrifices, and prayers are regarded as sacred by others. Hence it is reasonable for a person to refrain from judging any religion, even his own, until he has experienced it as a meaningful expression of real devotion.

III. Holy Orders and Sacred Scriptures

Holy Men and Women

THE origin and etymology of the terms *"religio"* and *"religiosus"* are obscure. They are probably Latin derivatives from a Greek verb meaning "to be mindful or careful," but whatever the original meaning may have been, we know that the actual meaning of these terms has changed often. It is impossible to give a clear definition of "religion" and "the religious life." It is even more difficult to get a general agreement among the religions concerning which institutions and traditions should properly be called religions. "Religion" is a Roman word and concept; even the Greeks had no word for it.

In late Roman times the term *religiosus* was applied to a person who was segregated from civil society and dedicated to a life of special devotions: hermits, ascetics, visionaries, mystics, mendicants, pilgrims—a variety of devotees who, by isolated disciplines, possessed or were seeking to obtain a purification from the evils of the world which they had renounced. Such segregation of individuals, voluntary or involuntary, for a complete devotion to religious observances has been a common feature of almost all cultures. These men and women are said to be consecrated or holy, and such dedication is commonly said to be an act of self-sacrifice.

Even the most primitive cultures have men and women who are recognized as having sacred talents and professions: medicine men, shamans, seers, sadhus, fakirs, all are recognized as having special powers and as competent to perform special services. Among these services are healing, prophesying, purifying, blessing, cursing, and invoking uncanny powers for good or evil. A Roman *religiosus*, however, was respected not so much for such services as for having a special devoutness or character. There was a peculiar privacy as well as privation in the life of a *religiosus*. Though outcast and exiled, he was respected and even venerated; many devotees were officially sanctified as saints. Theoretically they were living in another world, in communion with uncommon, invisible powers.

As the Roman Empire grew the number of these devotees increased, feeling the need to escape from the decadence of Roman society. Gradually these hermits banded together and shared some of their experiences. Informal associations led to formal communities or "wilderness sects." Such communities found shelter in caves or crude dwellings; they established regulations and orders for their devotions. Among Christians of Asia Minor and Eastern Europe such ascetic communities, with the support of their bishops, rapidly achieved prestige. Large monastic buildings were provided for monks and nuns. During feudal times, for various reasons, Christian monasticism flourished.

The people of Israel and Islam were not conceived as being religious in this Roman sense, though both peoples had their share of "wilderness" experience. These peoples were holy in the sense of having special divine laws and guidance. Gradually, however, among both peoples there developed outside the theocratic sacred union or covenant a few segregated religious groups and communities. Around Jerusalem, partly under Roman influence, there flourished desert communities, such as the Essenes in the caves above the Dead Sea, who kept aloof in order to cultivate their own, more intimate forms of piety. And later, within Islam this tendency toward pietistic rites and communities led to the organization of small fraternities of *sufis*. Out of these pious brotherhoods there grew holy orders and monasteries, which became increasingly popular as Islam moved eastward and conquered peoples among whom such segregated orders were common. For several centuries *sufism* was a powerful influence within the larger community of Islam. In Iran and India *sufi* sects are still active.

Monasticism

Among Christians and Buddhists monasticism developed at
about the same time, but for different reasons. Both types have
become major influences in the religious world.

The Greek monasteries of Asia Minor were built into regular
institutions under the initiative of Eustathius and the support of
Bishop Basil during the fourth century. St. Basil, especially, did
much to bring order and respectability to Eastern monasticism.
Believing that religion was essentially social, he subordinated
the monastic orders to the administration of the bishops. His
regimen for the monks provided not only regular daily devotions
and an ascetic diet, but also regular labor and study. The
monks were not only encouraged to practice "perpetual adoration" but were also trained as schoolmasters. Monasteries became not only refuges but also institutions of charity. During the
Tatar invasions the monasteries also became fortresses. Such
social and military services endeared the monks to the populace.
Monasteries became centers of pilgrimage and beneficiaries of
large endowments. The Macedonian monastery on Mount Athos
was one of the largest, and it assembled a famous library. The
studies of these monks took a mystic turn. A more scholastic
monastery was founded in Constantinople and was called the
Studium; it produced great hymns and beautiful manuscripts.
The most famous Russian monasteries were established at Kiev
in the eleventh century (the Pechersky Monastery) and near
Moscow in the fourteenth century (the Troitsa or Trinity Monastery). From the ranks of the monks or celibates came the
bishops and higher clergy.

From the East monasticism spread westward. Following the
barbarian invasions it spread rapidly through the Roman prov-
inces. Early in the sixth century St. Benedict and his sister,
Ste. Scholastica, founded the Benedictine Order of monks and
nuns. They established the famous monastery of Monte Cassino
near Rome. There the Roman Senator Cassiodorus established
the collection of manuscripts which the monks copied. The
Benedictines take a life-long vow of obedience, poverty, and

chastity; they abstain from meat and are confined within the monastic premises. About four hours of their day are devoted to public prayers and chanting, four hours to manual labor, and four hours to private study and meditation. The Augustinian cloistered communities were founded at the same time as the Benedictines and with a similar regimen. As in the East, these monasteries became fortresses. Among the most famous fortress-monasteries are Monserrat in Spain; St. Pierre of Ghent, Belgium; St. Albans in England; and Mont St. Michel in Brittany.

By the tenth century the monasteries had become not only centers of security amid the incessant wars of the time, but also wealthy cultural centers, and the strict discipline and ascetic ideals of the Benedictine Rules had relaxed. The abbots of the great House of Cluny in central France took the initiative in promoting reform and spiritual revival. It spread over wide regions of feudal society and affected both the Benedictine and Augustinian orders. It also led to the founding of still stricter orders, the Carthusians in 1086, and the Cistercians in 1098. In the Carthusian orders vows of silence were added to the older disciplines. When the monk Hildebrand became Pope Gregory the VIIth, he tried to make the Cluny reforms general and to revive the intensive devotional exercises of the monasteries. He also subordinated the Church's temporal powers, which had become great, to its spiritual powers.

The history of Buddhist monasticism tells a different story. Gautama Buddha, who as a young prince in northern India had fled the palace to adopt the wandering life of an ascetic *sadhu*, achieved his "Great Enlightenment" or discovery of the Middle (moderate) Way of devotion. As he gained disciples he formed a community. Tradition dates this event to 525 B.C. During the prolonged rainy season the early assemblies of monks were held in cave shelters. The communities thus formed were organized into orders of monks and nuns, and gradually monastic buildings took the place of the early shelters. The communion among the monks and nuns became recognized as one of the three essentials or "Jewels" of Buddhism, The Lord Buddha, his *dharma* (The Noble Eightfold Path), and the *Sangha*, the holy orders governed by the *Dharma*. These monks and nuns as they went about teaching and begging attracted large groups of sympathizers, but few of them took the monastic vows. This led to the recognition of Buddhist laymen, who observed as much of the Middle Way as they could in civil communities. However these lay Buddhists were required to enter a monastery for a specified period and to submit temporarily to all the regulations of the discipline. In this way Buddhism succeeded in transforming the rigid Orders of early monasticism into the more popular "middle way" of Buddhism as it developed in China and Japan. But even in this more popular form, the "great wheel" of Buddhism, the monastic orders are still an essential element, and are primarily responsible for placing Buddhism among the great religions of mankind.

Other Religious Orders

It is evident from this bit of religious history that the concept of the religious life developed everywhere a less exclusive idea of religious devotions than was required during the early history of monasticism. Even within monastic walls the religious life gained in cultural content and social interest. The rituals of both the Christian and Buddhist monastic orders became enriched by the arts of music, poetry, and painting, as well as by scholarship and devotional literature. Monks who had the competence were encouraged to substitute liberal arts for manual labor. Copying valuable ancient manuscripts, writing commentaries on them, and illuminating them with miniature decoration, learning the chants, all became normal monastic occupations and devotions. The blending of the two gave rise to the dictum: *laborare est orare* (work, too, is prayer).

In 1205 the Pope authorized a Spanish nobleman, Dominic, who had become an Augustinian monk, to leave the monastery and devote himself to teaching and preaching among the heretics of southern France. This led to the founding of the great Dominican Order of teachers, whose most noted member was St. Thomas Aquinas. Meanwhile, in Italy a young nobleman, Francis of Assisi, renounced his military duties and feudal estate to follow a wandering life of poverty, working, singing, preaching to the poor and communing with nature. He, too, was authorized to establish an Order. Soon many Franciscan friars were devoting their lives to helping the poor. Both the Dominicans and Franciscans founded "tertiary" orders of lay-men who dedicated themselves to charitable and benevolent activities. Similarly some Augustinians in the Netherlands founded benevolent orders of lay men and women which called themselves Friends of God, engaged in *Devotio Moderna.*

During the sixteenth and seventeenth centuries a variety of religious Orders were established. Among them were: The Teatines, who provided retreats for the regular clergy; The Oratorians, who developed the arts of high mass and liturgies with sacred music, and who taught and practiced the arts of preaching; The Ursulines, young women who befriended girls and acted as advisers; The Visitandes, a sisterhood that culti-vated both pious contemplation and acts of charity; The Lazaristes, who visited hospitals and prisons; The Society of Jesus (Jesuits), who became one of the most influential Orders and leaders in Roman Catholicism.

Let this bit of history suffice to suggest some general re-flections on genuine religion and on the attempts that indi-viduals and institutions make to devote their whole lives to religious observances. A professional devotee is a pathetic char-acter and not a saint. When holiness becomes an objective in-stead of a quality of life it becomes fanatical. Whether human beings live in solitude or in association, they must devote them-selves to concrete goods and not to devotion in general. The idea of giving one's whole life to God is a common and in-telligible religious motivation and confession, but in attempting to do this literally and physically men soon learn that religious devotion, however fundamental it may be, must be accompanied by other activities and secular devotions. Isolated, exclusive, "pure" and continuous religious exercises become insane. The in-stitution of Holy Orders has met this passion and guided it into constructive channels and worthy work, without renouncing the ideal of wholehearted devotion. Religion cannot live on and by itself; it must be related to other concerns. The history of holy men and holy orders makes this quite clear.

Or, to put this into ecclesiastical language, the "regular" and the "secular" clergy (monks and priests) need each other and both need laymen. It is not impossible or impractical to make religion a professional concern and to be a *religiosus* in the Roman sense. But even a professional religious person, a clergyman, cannot live on worship alone, anymore than he can live "on bread alone." This discovery is made in all religions, practically if not theoretically. In short, holiness is a virtue if it is not a passion but an incentive to work devotedly. It is well enough for the abbots to tell their monks and nuns that "work, too, is prayer," but this was not meant too literally. Work and prayer are supplementary.

Sacred Scriptures

As we have examined the relations between Holy Orders and daily life, so we must learn to relate sacred scriptures to literature. Sometimes these scriptures are good reading matter, especially for devotional reading, but they were not intended for this purpose. Their important functions in religion are varied, and these functions must be understood, if one wishes to know what has made particular scriptures sacred. A few historical illustrations may serve to explain these functions:

1. *Law.* Many sacred texts are law books; they formulate the divine commands of an actual government of a people. The ancient Greeks distinguished between *themis,* sacred law (associated with a god, *theos*) and human legislation, *nomos*; both were law, but the sacred law was "established" (constitutional) whereas the laws made by legislatures or courts were subject to repeal. The *Torah* of the Hebrews, the so-called Books of Moses, was the body of commands given by the people's covenanted Divine Lord. During the Captivity and after the destruction of the Temple in Jerusalem, much of this law could not be obeyed literally. But it continued to be holy as an object of devotion, even when some of it ceased to be literally law.

It is sacred for Jews, Christians, and Muslims. For Islam it is supplemented by the sacred Law Book, the *Qu'ran;* and for Christians by the books of the "New Covenant." The sacred *Dharma* of the Noble Eightfold Path is law for Buddhists. Usually such Law is sacred for a "chosen people" but many books of divine law are revered more generally as basic norms for religion rather than statute law for the civil community. This might be illustrated by the so-called Ten Commandments of the *Torah.* An early version of these commandments, related to agriculture and herding, reads about as follows (slightly abridged):

You shall make for yourselves no molten gods.
The feast of unleavened bread you shall keep.
All the first-born of your sons you shall redeem, and none shall appear before me empty.
Six days you shall work, but on the seventh day you shall rest. . . .
You shall observe the feast of weeks, the first fruits of wheat harvest, and the feast of ingathering at the end of the year.
Three times in the year shall all your males appear before the Lord God, the God of Israel. . . .
You shall not offer the blood of my sacrifice with leaven; neither shall the sacrifice of the Feast of the Passover be left until the morning.
The first of the first fruits of your ground you shall bring to the house of the Lord your God.
You shall not boil a kid in its mother's milk.

(*Exodus* 34: 17-26)

This was then supplemented by the less ritualistic Law:

You shall have no other gods before me.
You shall not make for yourselves a graven image. . . .
You shall not take the name of The Lord your God in vain. . . .
Remember the Sabbath Day, to keep it holy. . . .
Honor your father and your mother. . . .
You shall not kill.
You shall not commit adultery.
You shall not steal.
You shall not bear false witness against your neighbor.
You shall not covet . . . anything that is your neighbor's.

(*Exodus* 20: 3-17)

During the so-called Deuteronomic Reform there was added to these two types of commandments the *Shema,* which is the most sacred symbol still of Judaism and the central expression of its religious devotion:

> Hear, O Israel: The Lord our God, the Lord is One; and you shall love the Lord your God with all your heart, and with all your soul, and with all your might.
>
> And these words which I command you this day shall be upon your heart; and you shall teach them diligently to your children.
>
> (*Deuteronomy* 6:4-7)

To this "first and greatest" commandment was added:

> You shall love your neighbor as a being like yourself.
>
> (*Leviticus* 19:18)

Still later, the Prophet Micah expressed the spirit of the Law in these famous words:

> He has showed you, O man, what is good; and what does the Lord require of you but to do justice, love mercy, and walk humbly with your God.
>
> (*Micah* 6:8)

Such declarations of divine law are important parts of public worship. They are recited solemnly and regularly in the rituals or they may be chanted. The *Torah* is also expounded and interpreted in the *Talmuds* of the rabbis, who explain which parts are still literally law for the Jewish communities and which are to be revered as sacred tradition though they cannot be obeyed as law.

2. *Rituals.* Sacred scriptures include public forms of prayer, praise, sacrifices, dances, meditations, sacraments, and rites for special occasions. Many of these are chants or hymns. For example, many of the Psalms in the Bible were chants used in the Temple at Jerusalem. Many of the great *sutras* of the Buddhists are intoned by the monks to the accompaniment of

gongs. There is a famous and very ancient hymn in the *Rig Veda* of the Aryans which was chanted at the sacrifices by the Brahmans around the domestic hearths, and which then became a subject for meditation and philosophical commentary:

> There was then neither nonbeing nor being;
> There was no air nor sky beyond.
> What was then hidden? Wherein? For whom?
> And was there deep, unfathomable water?
>
> ....
>
> First there was darkness by darkness hidden,
> Without distinctions all was water.
> Covered by the void there came into being
> The ONE, impelled by heat.
> In the Beginning desire entered into the ONE;
> It was the primal seed, product of thought.
> Sages searching wisely in their hearts
> Disclosed the bond of being and nonbeing.
>
> ....
>
> Who knows surely? Who can say it?
> Whence born, whence came this creation?
> Not till afterwards were the gods born,
> Then who can know whence creation arose?
> No one knows whence creation arose,
> And whether he made it or not.
> He who sees in the highest heaven,
> He only knows.—Or does he?
>
> (*Rig Veda*, Hymn No. X)

There is another famous hymn, composed in the third century B.C. by the Greek philosopher, Cleanthes; it may not have been part of any ritual, but it became a classic expression of the meditations of the Stoics:

> O Zeus! Thou art praised above all gods;
> Many are thy names, Thou the Almighty forever.
> The beginning of the world was from Thee;
> And with Law dost Thou rule over all things.
> Unto Thee all mankind may speak;
> For thine offspring are we all.
> Hence I raise my hymn to Thee;

And will ever sing of thy power.
The heavenly system obeys thy word
As it circles above the earth.
The lesser and the great lights mingle;
How great art Thou, eternal King over all.
Nothing on earth is done without Thee,
Nor in the heavens, nor in the seas,
Except the deeds of the evil in their folly.
But thine art makes even the crooked straight;
The formless has form for Thee, and the alien is akin.
Thou hast fitted all together,
The good with the evil;
That thy word should be one in all,
World without end.
Take folly from our souls,
That we may return to Thee the honor that Thou
Hast granted unto us;
Praising thy works forever
As is fitting for human kind.

                    (Taken from Stobaeus)

3. *Myth.* Myths are often incorporated into rituals, but they have a religious significance as sacred scriptures apart from their use in public worship. There are many secular myths that grow out of cultural history and political experience and that take the form of folk-lore, epic poems, and heroic records. But religious myths are different: they are basic materials of religious instruction in narrative form, and they have a more direct relation to religious devotion than have legends and folklore. They may deal with historical material in allegorical or fabulous form, or they may be purely imaginative. A myth is neither a story nor a history. It is more: it imparts a serious theme in story form. The myth of the fall of Adam and Eve, for example, dramatizes the passage of human beings from innocence to conscience. The myth of Buddha's enlightenment under the bo-tree, describes the rebellion of the middle castes against the extreme asceticism of the Brahmans. The myth of the Pure Land, in certain schools of Buddhism, portrays the ease with which the faithful can pass from "the wheel of birth and death"; and this "wheel" gives a mythical expression to the course of human experience. The many myths of creation give

history a beginning and an end, thus a basic theme or meaning.

A myth does not explain a fact; it gives form to a faith. For this reason it is foolish to detach a myth from its context. It is equally foolish to try to rob a living faith of its cherished mythical expressions and images. It is true, to be sure, that with the lapse of time and change of cultures a myth may survive its religious uses and become secular folklore. Myths, like all other arts, have their careers and eventually lose their religious power and relevance. But an educated devotion needs a rich rhetoric and poetic imagination to make itself articulate and intellectually meaningful.

Sacred scriptures are seldom compositions by individual authors; they bring together, often casually, much traditional material and local idioms. The essential message of a gospel in most religions is not put into didactic language, but is given the more impressive forms of parable, fable, miracle, and myth. Not all these materials have the same sacred status or the same devotional significance. A drama like *Prometheus Bound* had the importance for Greek religion that the poem of Job has for Hebrew-Christian prophecy; the powerful religious content surpasses the question of authorship. Myths are not easily or significantly transportable from one religion into another, though they are important contributions to the literary heritage of mankind. The literature of myth gives to morals a temporal dimension and gives to time an imaginative meaning; but the devotional uses of myth are less universal.

4. *Prophecy.* This universality is even more true of prophecy. Prophetic scriptures are human attempts to speak with authority, that is, to report the Voice of God. Prophets have heard God, and announce: Thus saith the Lord. The contents of such announcements vary considerably. Some of them are warnings, some predictions, some condemnations, some commandments, some praises, some comforts, and some are visions of doom— "apocalyptic prophecies." Major prophets, though they usually addressed a particular people in a time of crisis, are listened to by many generations of many peoples, when they need to hear an authoritative voice.

Prophetic writings, even more than myths, are apt to be couched in a highly personal rhetoric and are made to sound oracular. But above all, major prophets have a sense of tragedy; they are able to see through human existence rather than into the future.

Although the Greeks developed the art of prophecy and the concept of prophecy very differently from the Hebrews, their religious thinking was deeply involved in the contrast between *prometheus* (foresight) and *epimetheus* (hindsight). Much more important to them than their popular oracles, were the great festivals when they heard the tragedies composed by their poets. These dramas, from Aeschylus's *Prometheus Bound* to Euripides's *Trojan Women,* were the central expression of their religious thought and experience; they have remained classics of prophetic literature and tragic insight into human life. They are also excellent examples of the religious use of myth.

5. *Wisdom Literature.* Lastly, the sacred books also usually contain a miscellany of writings, the reflections of sages, moral teachers, or religious poets. These are frankly human compositions, but they are compositions which, for one reason or another, have been cherished by many generations. They are not exactly sacred but they are "authentic wisdom."

Devotional Writings

In some religions there is a sharp line drawn between the canonical books that are sacred because they are divine revelation and other writings that have been essential contributions to a religious tradition and are revered but not regarded as holy. Saints, sages, poets have provided a heritage of religious literature that has been important for more than one religion and therefore represents a part of the heritage of mankind. The Buddhists, Zoroastrians, Jews, Christians, Muslims, Sikhs have canons of sacred authority. In Hinduism, Confucianism, Taoism, Shintoism, and the religions of ancient Egypt, Greece, and Rome no rigid line is drawn between holy books and others. In the former group there is an attempt to define orthodoxy and heresy;

in the latter, this is impossible. There is a fairly clear distinction between pious devotional literature and the writings of the mystics, but the term "mysticism" is now used so indiscriminately, that the historical distinctions between pietism and mysticism are obscured. It would be idle to enter upon a classification of the great wealth and variety of devotional literature.

The Christian monasteries were, as we have pointed out earlier, especially significant as treasure houses of sacred and devotional writings and as centers of the religious use of such books. Before the invention of printing any book was precious, but in the monasteries devotional books were doubly precious. The adoration of medieval monks can still be seen and felt by anyone who examines monastic libraries and the "illumination" of sacred scriptures, liturgies, prayerbooks, and other materials of devotional exercises. An outstanding product of the monasteries is *The Golden Legend*. The version which has become a classic is the book by this title compiled by a bishop of Genoa, Jacobus de Voragine, who was ordained as a Dominican in 1244. It is a collection of lives of the saints with commentary on the Christian Calendar and especially on saints' days. It was early translated into the modern languages and was second only to the Bible in circulation and devotional use. The English edition was made (with variations) by William Caxton, who was the first English printer.

IV. Sanctuaries, Shrines and Temples

HAVING surveyed the patterns of devotion in holy living, holy orders, and sacred scriptures, we come next to holy places. Like the other aspects of devotion, holy places are dedicated. Whether or not their origin as sanctified places rests on a formal rite of dedication, they are places that are reserved and respected as areas for some kind of religious activity or act of piety and as sacred to some object of worship or to rites of devotion. A sanctuary may serve any one or more of various religious functions, but on it or in it there is always some visible sign of a sacred presence. Invisible beings are often called "spirits," but human beings usually have good reasons for representing their presence by visible representations or symbols, and by making the sacred area appear worthy of its spiritual resident.

Places of Refuge

Just as there are areas publicly reserved and marked as wild-life sanctuaries or bird refuges, or deer parks, so in many primitive, and in some not so primitive cultures there are human refuges. Such refuges are sacred in the sense that no act of violence is permitted in them. Thus persons who are fleeing from enemies or punishment are given an opportunity (usually fairly distant) where they can find peace. Here and there groves, that used to be peaceful, sacred sanctuaries and communities, are shown to tourists. One such remnant of a sanctuary can be seen near Hilo, Hawaii. It is still a quiet park along the coast, but it no longer serves as a sanctuary as it did a century or two ago, when "civilized" powers had not yet abolished it as contrary to law and order. In many cultures, however, it has been regarded as a sacred obligation to provide a place, besides prisons, of physical security. Whatever miscellany of inhabitants managed to escape to such refuges were compelled to live in peace and quiet with each other. In this way the sanctuaries functioned as monasteries, much as monasteries on occasion functioned as refuges. Usually a refugee did not spend much of his life in such a place, for he found some other means of escape from trouble; men usually prefer exile to being inviolable inmates of a refuge.

Tombs

A grave, with some symbol of honor or memorial on it, has a kind of sanctity and is, for this reason, usually protected from trespass or walled into a public cemetery. Some cemeteries are called "church-yards" because church members have been honored by burial in or near the church. But graveyards do not owe their sanctity to the church; they are intrinsically holy places. Graves are not holy to everyone, but each grave is holy to some one who cherishes the memory of the deceased. Burial cults are among the oldest forms of religion that the archeologists have discovered.

A tomb is made to be durable and usually contains either a durable monument or durable memorials buried with the corpse. In most cultures the private burial rites are supplemented by community memorial rites, which usually combine secular and religious forms of celebration. The *Bon* dances of the Japanese are good examples of such ceremonies. In addition to their secular features, they require the ceremonial erecting of a temporary holy place for the annual honoring of the dead. These rites are very popular for a variety of reasons and mark the high point of the Japanese religious calendar.

In ancient Rome, tombs were built architecturally like houses and furnished as residences for the dead, even though the majority of Romans did not believe that the spirits of the dead were entombed. Similarly in Egypt the ancient tombs of notables were the burial places not only of their bodies but of their treasures; and this devotional obligation led to the most monumental efforts to make tombs places of security. But in Egypt, as also in some of the oldest tombs discovered in Europe, there was always an escape hole for the spirit.

In many early cultures, and even today, roaming spirits are feared and there are special rites and prayers for inducing the spirits of the deceased to "stay at rest." The fear of being haunted is one of the elements that explain the elaborate provisions made religiously for the entombed, as well as the elaborate funeral pomp of the burial cultus.

Residences for Ancestral Spirits

One of the common features of piety in the Far East is the provision made in the homes of the living for a permanent abode of the ancestral spirits. Accompanying such shrines in the living rooms of the family (which usually take the form of small memorial tablets of wood placed on the "ancestor shelf") there are simple but eloquent rites such as daily and devoutly placing small bowls of rice and a few flowers before the ancestral tablets, burning incense, and bidding the spirits to feel at home with their posterity. The way in which such ceremonies make the fellowship of several generations sensibly real is illustrated by the following typical prayer which the eldest son addresses to the deceased father:

> Alas, my father, thou hast been taken from us. I, and the others that remain behind will continue to do thee faithful service in our hearts. Thy life has come to its close on earth. Hear us in thy place of rest as we celebrate thy obsequies. Deign, exalted spirit, to take up thine abode in this memorial tablet, and remain at rest forever in this thy house. I address thee with the deepest reverence.
>
> I prayed day and night that thou mightest live to be a hundred years old, and now I can but weep and lament that thou hast left this beautiful world and gone to the dark land beyond. I beseech thee, listen in peace to us thy relatives assembled here as we celebrate the worship of the deceased.
>
> Our prayer is that thou wilt lie down to rest in the grave, leaving thy spirit behind thee to guard the house. Reverently and with humility I make this prayer to thy spirit which has now become divine.

The heart of piety is the consciousness that the living are a minority. In a religious community or family many generations exist together, a few in body and many in spirit. The presence of the absent is one of the basic insights of religion.

Shrines

Images or icons encased in appropriate shrines and representing holy beings is one of the most widespread and popular forms of devotional expression. In addition to such domestic shrines as have been described above, small shrines to gods, saints, or local guardian spirits are placed at the crossroads or street corners or in gardens, wherever those who pass or dwell can offer a few flowers and say a prayer. In some of the sacred cities of India, like Benares, pilgrims laden with baskets of flowers and pots of water go from one street corner to the next, pausing at each shrine to place a few flowers and sprinkle a little water on the images.

Shrines are also assembled in sacred buildings; the rites of reverence at each shrine are usually very simple, but the buildings become fantastically elaborate. For example, the great Buddhist holy places are not temples but huge collections of shrines. These stupas or pagodas were erected over a central shrine containing some relic of a buddha or bodhisattva. The early shrines contained no human images but only symbols of Buddhist doctrine: wheel, tree, lion, lotus, etc. Gradually, however, they were surrounded by hundreds of images and varied shrines. Such Buddhist monuments are among the most notable centers of devotion: Sanchi Stupa (India), Shwe Dagon Pagoda (Rangoon, Burma), Ananda Monastery (Pagan, Burma), Angkor Wat (Cambodia), Wat Arun (Bangkok, Thailand), Nara (Japan), and Borobodur (Java, Indonesia).

Altars

An altar is a place for ceremonial sacrifices, accompanied by prayers. Sacrifices are usually either thank-offerings or petitions. Altars may be created unceremoniously in the height of an emotional occasion, or the domestic hearth may be sanctified by routine sacrifices and thus become an altar before it serves its secular functions. In any case, an altar is theoretically not a table.

There is a story that comes down from ancient Greece about a group of survivors from a shipwreck, who, in addition to building fires on the shore for warming and drying themselves, built a ceremonial fire for sacrifices of thanksgiving. A Stoic philosopher who chanced to be passing asked them: Where are the altars of the drowned? This rhetorical question is taken by the critics of conventional religion or by those who have never been shipwrecked to be a reasonable satire of sacrifices. But the real point of the story is that the man who ridiculed the thanksgiving had obviously not been on the ship. Such wisecracks are incredibly childish or callous. The altars had not been erected to the Stoic divinity of universal providence, but to some god for his particular providence. The altars of the survivors were expressive of both thanksgiving and mourning. Even a hardened sailor among the survivors would have understood the propriety of the altar and joined in the sacrifice, for though he may have been hardened to storms and sacrifices, a survival from a shipwreck was an event that demanded observance. Sailors, fishers and farmers become hardened to bad weather, but do not express their emotions by cursing at storms and ruined crops. Only a fool or a Stoic or a foolish Stoic would remain unruffled by a spectacular good fortune. In a crisis there are naturally and decently spontaneous prayers and improvised altars, not for showing fear, but gratitude.

However, the altars which we must examine next are not for emergencies; they are formalized and institutionalized; they are standardized equipment for regular devotions. They are not primitive or rustic holy places under trees, but "high altars" in temples. These formalized altars with their sacrifices and prayers are for the use of those persons or communities that are aware of many and continual reasons for both thanksgiving and petition, and that regard it as appropriate and decent to make general provision for acknowledging these general circumstances.

Devotions at such altars may be less emotional, more reflective; less personal, more public. To appreciate such altars and observances we must examine them as public services.

Temples

A temple is a public residence for the Holy Spirit of a community or communion. For public devotions it is necessary to have the presence of the Being to whom public worship is addressed. In a temple a congregation assembles to face not each other but the invisible presence of the holy. And when individuals enter a temple for private devotions, they are doing so because they need the public invisible presence. A temple must be exalted in clear contrast to the homes of the worshippers. A temple is more than a place for formal devotions and more than a great shrine. By its proportions, symbols, arts, and rites it is supposed to be "heavenly," a place where the divine presence is public; it should have the power of carrying the minds, imaginations, and emotions of those who enter and worship there into another world, where the glory of God takes the place of the world of toil.

Thus temples do in a more direct and powerful way what sacred scriptures are also intended to do. Temples are the creation of the inspired and cooperative devotion of all the arts. To a hard-pressed tourist a temple in all its complexity of holy darkness, echoing chants, sculptures, images, colors, candles and altars is apt to be bewildering or stunning rather than imposing. But to the sunburned farmer who enters it from the fields it is transporting; it takes him out of his working world and into the eternal dimensions of being. He is not supposed to feel at home in it; but it is his refuge and sanctuary. He knows the meanings of its symbols and rites and can adjust himself to living for a short time in another world. This is not so much a place of rest as of restoration; it allows repose to the body, but the mind and imagination are far off and up. And if he desires, he can make his private devotions in this house of God.

V. Religious Expressions and Symbols

A WELL-CONSTRUCTED and well-placed temple or altar or shrine or image or tomb is an example of the fine art of symbolical architecture. Holy structures and areas should appear to be sanctified; they must be silently meaningful, expressing by their form their religious functions. Religion in general, like religious architecture, as a part of civilized society has the opportunity as well as the obligation to give the imaginative richness of civilized devotion a worthy embodiment. Good religion, in other words, needs the cooperation of the fine arts. It takes a variety of symbolical forms to give religious experience adequate expression. Therefore a seriously religious person must be able to comprehend how devotional language, symbols, music, and structures convey the spirit of devotion effectively. As in life generally, he needs critical appreciation and good judgment. A religion can not be understood critically by its immediate esthetic surface nor by a prosaic interpretation of its language. The right enjoyment of good religion requires the ability to see more than meets the eye and to hear more than strikes the ear.

The Language and Posture of Prayer

Let us first examine from this point of view one of the basic forms of religious expression, the saying of prayers. To be genuinely expressive a prayer must be accompanied by emotion, reflection, and purpose. A formal, public prayer has the difficult task of generalizing both language and attitude. For example: the Collect that opens the Anglican Order for Holy Communion begins:

> Almighty God, unto whom all hearts are open, all desires known, and from whom no secrets are hid; cleanse the thoughts of our

hearts by the inspiration of Thy Holy Spirit, that we may perfectly love Thee.

The basic theme of this eloquent language and formal petition
is the desire to be perfectly honest and sincere. A person who
cannot join in this prayer, though he may not find its style
congenial nor its poetry familiar, must harbor some uncleanness
or insincerity that makes his "love" "imperfect." The technical
and traditional Christian diction of "Almighty God," "Holy
Spirit," "inspiration," "cleanse" and "hearts" enhances the prayer
for Christians, and need not obstruct the devotion of an outsider who may wish to face a perfect judge. This is a public
form and generalized formulation to introduce the sacrament
of personal confession and petition; it provides an opportunity
for each communicant to search his own "heart."

Similarly in "A General Thanksgiving" the Prayer Book provides the following, introductory form:

> Father of all mercies, we, Thine unworthy servants do give Thee
> most humble and hearty thanks for all Thy goodness and loving-
> kindness to us and to all men. We bless Thee for our creation,
> preservation, and all the blessings of this life.

This is so general a thanksgiving to "the Father of all mercies"
(not to Almighty God) for "all Thy goodness" (not for every-
thing) that it is verbally redundant and intellectually innocent.
It specifies "all the blessings of this life" but it does not (yet)
enumerate. The thanksgiving is purely formal but also purely
clear. It expresses elegantly an opportunity for anyone to be
thankful for any mercy or blessing that he has received and that
others may have received. It ought to suggest an awareness of
particular blessings by particular grateful persons, but these, of
course, are not for public enumeration.

However, the general thanksgiving proceeds to mention a
few blessings that are presumably general for all Christian communicants. Here an outsider, if he happened to wish to share
in the general thanksgiving, might wish to make reservations.
The formula was clearly not intended for him, after the first

paragraph, but it at least gives him an opportunity to make up his mind about his particular blessings.

The religious language of prayers, meditations, sacrifices, and other formal devotions is most effective and appropriate when it gives to an individual a consciousness and expression of vaguely felt needs, desires, guilt, hopes, or whatever experiences might otherwise be unformulated though real, in his actual life of devotion. But public forms abuse their useful function when they impose some particular content that ought to be supplied by the communicant himself. Public forms are reasonable and helpful when they assist the communicant in being articulate, without imposing insincerity on him.

The gestures and postures, such as kneeling, prostration, bowing, which are conventional symbols of devotion, meditation, prayer, are ways of creating a general environment for public forms. But more especially they symbolize the invisible presence of a Holy Spirit, or a perfect judge, or a general benevolence, "under" whom the religious rites are performed. Public devotions are apt to be lifeless if this invisible presence is not emotionally tangible and imaginatively real.

Included in this symbolical art is the use of a sacred vocabulary of hallowed expressions. These cannot well be universal so long as there is no universal language and culture. The plurality of religions is necessary where there is a plurality of traditions and cultures, for it is impossible to have a "living" religion in a cultural vacuum. There are some concepts and metaphors that several religions may share, but the common concepts may receive different interpretations. This is true even within a single religion, for symbolical language is usually meaningful rather than precise. Such ideas as: the last day of judgment, eternal life, heavenly kingdom, "Thine is the Glory," "Amen," etc. are essential to a well-developed religion. And they contribute a kind of symbolical concreteness which public forms demand, without the kind of definition and fixity which they would need if they were used in knowledge rather than in praise and prayer. Such forms enable a wealth of private meanings to find public embodiment.

Confession

One of the most basic of these forms is the language of ritual confession, the language of sin and salvation. Feeling guilt, being lost or unclean are common emotional and moral states that call not only for analysis and clarification and remedy, but first of all for expression. The religious forms of expression are not analytic; they are mythic and rhetorical and graphic; they have genuine power as expressive media, though they explain nothing. They express needs rather than cures. The seeking for salvation, enlightenment, deliverance, assurance, forgiveness, which is at the heart of the most intense religious experience, demands first of all to be confessed, made articulate not for some other person but for the seeker himself. To confess in some kind of public formula expresses what has been repressed, and this is a first step in relief. In this sense, religion is an excellent opiate, when a good opiate is needed. The attempts on the part of religious organizations to make diagnoses and provide remedies are often less effective and reasonable. But psychiatry, too, finds the problems of cure more difficult than the theory of diagnosis. Comforters are not healers, but they may be needed and may help. In any case, the primary aim of religious confessions and devotions is not medical. Religion raises more problems than it solves, but it is useful in raising them and in joining the secular arts when they seek remedies.

Purification Rites

This may become more concrete if we examine a well-developed purification rite, which, though it purifies nothing, contributes significantly to enjoying life. The Great National Purification Festival of Shinto is celebrated annually in Japan as follows:

In preparation for the Purification each member of the community is supplied with a bit of paper by the Shinto priests. It is cut into the stylized shape of a human figure. Ceremonially it must be rubbed over the whole body, whereby the accumulated transgressions and impurities are symbolically transferred to the paper homunculus. The papers are then collected by the priests, tied into bundles according to traditional specifications, and then heaped on a decorated platform in a sacred precinct or near a river bank. The decorated area and platform thus laden with the guilt of the whole community are known as "the purification ground." Meanwhile the rituals of purification are being performed at the temple or shrine. Food offerings are made to the spirits, followed by prayers and a proclamation of absolution, as follows:

> Hearken everyone to the Great Purification by which at this year's sixth month Heaven deigns to purge and absolve all manner of faults and transgressions.
>
> Now of the various faults and transgressions committed by the celestial race destined more and more to people this land, some are against Heaven, to wit, the breaking down of hedges between rice fields, filling up of irrigation ditches, removing water pipes, sowing seed over again, skinning animals alive or backwards. These are known as offenses against heaven.
>
> Earthly offenses are: committing such acts as cutting living bodies, cutting up dead bodies, leprosy, incest, bestiality, calamities caused by creeping things, by the spirits on high, by birds high in flight, sorcery.
>
> Whenever these are committed let the Great Spirit, in accordance with the custom of the Heavenly Palace, cut saplings of sacred trees, top and bottom, and make thereof a whole row for a thousand stands for offerings. Then let him recite the mighty words of the celestial ritual. When he does so, the heavenly spirits, opening wide the adamantine door of Heaven and cutting through the thick-piled clouds with an awful blow, will lend ear. The earth spirits, climbing to the tops of the high mountains and to the hill tops, sweeping away the mists from the mountains and hills, will lend ear.
>
> When they have thus lent ear, all offenses whatsoever will be annulled, from the Court of the Sovereign Divine Descendant to the provinces of the four quarters under Heaven. As the high-piled clouds of Heaven are scattered by the breath of the Wind-Spirits; as the morning breezes and the evening breezes clear away the fogs; as yonder thicket of brush is chopped down and cleared away by the sharp sickle forged in the fire, so shall offenses

be utterly annulled. The divine spirits of the tides and seas will swallow them. The blowing spirits of the winds will blow them to the Bottomland.

Then the papers are loaded onto a barge, gayly decorated with branches and lanterns. The barge is towed out to sea and sunk with the accompaniment of the people's great rejoicing.

Of course, when this rite happens to follow the usual spring housecleaning and garden trimming, or an epidemic, the national ceremony has the additional value of celebrating days of drudgery or suffering. But even when the symbolism of removing the ills from the body is pure formality, though reminiscent of primitive magic, such a formality gains meaning by being a part of the great national festival of rejoicing and of the feeling of beginning again with "a clean slate."

Praise

The art of symbolism and expression reaches its greatest height in the composition and rendering of hymns of praise and psalms to accompany sacrifices or thanks offerings. The attributes of God and other religious language of praise exceed all doctrine and become extravagant in the efforts to glorify God. Sacred music is genuinely poetical and exalted. Haydn's celebration of "a new created world" in his oratorio, *The Creation,* was a fine expression not only of Christian joy but also of the current Newtonian enthusiasm.

Folk arts provide a very different but equally genuine medium for praise and joy. Indian folk dances (both Asian and American) are highly religious expressions. Festivals and "spirituals" in many cultures are intense emotional rites.

There have also been many horrible sacrifices, like those of the Mayas and Aztecs. And there are tragic conflicts of devotion, like Abraham's conflicting devotion to God and to his son, Isaac. The devotions of the great religions are full of tragic themes. Much of such celebration of tragedy is sublime art. However, religions, like the arts, are not all fine. Decadent, cruel, fanatical religions are among the greatest of evils. Re-

ligions become pathetic, too. The immense amount of senti-
mental, ignorant devotion is worse than no devotion. And the
so-called "sacred," so-called "music" of which the churches are
guilty is disgraceful. The crude and careless mixture of second-
rate folk art with third-rate religion is a common scandal.
Vulgarity and formalism are the opposite poles of religious vice,
and both are unfortunately conspicuous.

VI. Communion and Public Worship

Congregation

RELIGIOUS communities become established in many ways. The elaborate systems that prehistoric peoples and the so-called "primitive," illiterate peoples of today have used for uniting families, clans, tribes into villages, and villages into communities with government and morality is a very complicated story. And even more technical and complicated is the interpretation of the many ceremonies, customs, totems and taboos, that enter into this transformation. To understand them involves an analysis of the relations between laws, kinship structure, myths, magic, and beliefs about the powers that operate in the mysterious world about them. Attempts by anthropologists and archaeologists to guess how religion emerged out of this complex, and where to draw the line between magic and religion have been abandoned. Only a century ago the scientists were still teaching that fear created the gods. Now, the whole attempt to reconstruct the evolution of religion in general is too speculative to be useful. Different cultures lead to different conclusions. Therefore, instead of pretending that we know how religious communities and communions evolved, we do better to begin by examining the less speculative historical origins of the major religions today. And our first problem is to note how peoples formed religious congregations and communions out of secular communities and aggregations.

The term "congregation" may serve as a convenient word to designate any social structure that can be called a "religious body." A brief survey will show that different peoples have formed congregations in very different ways and understood them by very different theoretical interpretations.

In India two thousand years ago as well as today the inhabitants of villages have congregated around a holy man—Brahman priest, yogi, ascetic, or teacher (*guru*). Aged men of the upper castes are supposed to spend their last years in the pursuit of wisdom and in teaching the heritage of traditional wisdom. It has been and still is comfortable for Indian villagers to gather in the cool of the evening (and often for most of the night) under a tree at the edge of the village in order to hear a *guru*, a venerated old sage, tell or chant what he has learned. There is a voluminous and ancient literature of "forest treatises" and of commentaries on them (*upanishads*) that are the product of such a congregation of hearers of the oral tradition, and this literature still serves as the preferred basis for religious discussion. This is the foundation of Hindu religious tradition as a possession of communities. The term "Hinduism," by the way, is not known in India; it was created by foreigners and it gives the impression that the religious life and tradition of India has more structure and unity than it really has.

Those persons who wish more than this elementary and popular instruction may go to an *ashram*, a school conducted by a *guru*. Members of an *ashram* receive instruction and participate in discussion for several weeks, or months, or years, as they choose (subject to the *guru's* willingness to have them). A very distinguished leader of an *ashram* is often referred to as a *mahatma*. In this very flexible and informal way religious communities beyond the village congregations are formed. And the only orthodoxy that exists is the general consensus among *gurus* concerning whose teachings are tolerable. The only kind of establishment that so-called Hinduism has, centers in the temples and shrines. There are a few "missions" (notably the Ramakrishna Mission) which form their own congregations. There are also a few *samajes* or Religious Reform Societies; these were influential in the nineteenth century but now have a negligible rôle. The kind of religious literature that is most cherished depends largely on the tastes, needs, and abilities of the teachers. By far the most sacred and beloved religious classic today is the *Bhagavad-Gita* (Song of the Lord) which is taken from the great epic poem, the *Mahabharata*. This *Gita* was composed sometime between 200 B.C. and 200 A.D. and is now one of the world's classics of religious devotion. It presents Vishnu in the form of Krishna giving counsel to Prince Arjuna before battle concerning the three ways of duty and of deliverance: the way of knowledge (outlined by the Brahmans), the way of *yoga* (disciplines and duties), and the way of *bhakti* or devotion to a lord. Though all three ways are defended, it is clear that *bhakti* is recommended as the simplest and most available to all.

Mysteries

At the other extreme of congregational organization are the mysteries, which are open only to the initiates. The *yogis* of India have a few esoteric schools of this type, but these are exceptional. The most important and influential Mysteries were those of ancient Egypt, Greece, and Rome. The Grecian Mysteries (Dionysian, Eleusinian, Orphic, and others) were quite distinct from the public or civil cults of the Olympian deities. Each had its own secret rites and traditions. Scattered around the Mediterranean Sea during Roman times there were other such Mysteries, some entering from the East. Chief among them were the Mysteries of Isis, Mithra, Asklepios, and Magna Mater. The early Christian congregations had many of the features of a Mystery Religion: rites of initiation, purification, and regeneration. Members called themselves "Citizens of Heaven." Such mystery cults grew rapidly as the Roman Empire disintegrated, and they looked for a new heaven and a new earth.

Covenants

Among the most formal conceptions of an exclusive religious community was the myth of a covenant between a people and its God. This theocratic conception of a holy people legally under its God served to sanctify the political status of the people; it became a community consecrated as a whole to the service of its Lord. Such "chosen" people or congregations acknowledge the sovereignty of the divine law and subject themselves as well as their earthly rulers to it. Such a theory unites the secular and religious aspects of community and communion. The ancient Hebrews traced this kind of covenant to Abraham's covenant with his God, according to which the people promise to conform to the law of God, who in turn promises to protect and prosper the people. Islam and many Christian congregations adopted this theory of communion.

The early Christians linked this theory with the faith in a new covenant which prepared them for the New Jerusalem and for citizenship in heaven. As the Roman authority continued to collapse, the Christians looked forward to their entrance into the heavenly theocracy. But as new types of worldly authority developed, the theory of dual citizenship, in heaven and on earth, was gradually transformed into the theory of two kinds of power and authority: temporal and spiritual. The conflict between these two led to a long and bitter conflict between emperors and popes, between bishops and princes, between church and state. This conflict has confused and disturbed for centuries the relations between political loyalty and personal devotion to religious organizations. Similar problems arose for Judaism and Islam.

Synagogues

With the loss of the Temple in Jerusalem and the scattering of the Jewish communities throughout the civilized world, the rabbis were faced with the problem of reconciling the ancient Covenant with the new circumstances. As best they could, they obeyed and enforced the moral law. They substituted for the ritual law of the Temple a form of collective devotion to the law and a study of the law as an object of love. Out of this grew the synagogues, which had their origins in ancient times and which in medieval times became the civic and religious centers of Jewish communities. Prayerbooks took the place of sacrifices. The priesthood lost its power and the communities became thoroughly democratized, while clinging to their theocratic conception of the chosen people as a holy nation. In the synagogue the sanctuary contains the Ark, which contains the sacred scrolls of the Torah. The *Thirteen Principles of Faith* formulated by Maimonides in the early middle ages as a ritual creed, the ancient Eighteen Blessings now recited as a prayer, and medieval poems and hymns were gradually introduced into the Sabbath services of worship. Meanwhile the rabbis were compiling and composing a voluminous commentary or "fence" around the Torah. However, the most spontaneous center of devotion was the family circle, and the most popular and emotional form of communion was the Seder Feast (Passover).

Mosques and Sufis

The development of two different types of communion is noteworthy in Islam. When first formed by Muhammad in Mecca and Medina, the devoted band of his followers were a brotherhood of reformers united by a solemn law of submission, called *Islam*. This fraternity was devoted to putting an end to tribal strife among Arabs, first by mediation and then by combat. Islam was for males and soldiers only. As its conquests grew it had the responsibility of building a new social order. Within a few centuries it was imposing a sacred civilization on millions of men and women from Spain to Java. It had to adapt its law, the *Shi'a*, to many different cultures. In doing so it established a transnational, multicultural communion. In addition to a single law, it demanded a uniform schedule of public prayers. The prayers centered in great houses of communion, called mosques.

The religious power of Islam rests largely on this impressive international structure of public prayer. These universal rites of communion express the unity of a civilization, which exists more in ideal than in fact. For as Islam became a world power and a world religion it found itself unable to maintain the hope of a universal culture. The Muslim *Shi'a* had to adapt itself to a variety of peoples. Hence, within this overexpanded unity of faith there arose numerous local communions with their own intense devotions. Outstanding among these are the *sufis*, in whose communion the mystic love of God takes priority over the love of the law. A saintly woman of the eighth century expressed the *sufi* type of devotion in lines that became classic for the various *sufi* communities:

> My selfish love is that I do naught
> But think on Thee, excluding all beside;
> But that purest love, which is thy due,
> Is that thy veils fall, and I behold Thee,
> No praise to me in either this or that,
> Nay, Thine the praise for both that love and this.

This shift from communion to illumination in devotion became the central theme for the *sufi* pietists, and soon there were thousands meeting in small groups and showing the intensity of their "perfect love" in a variety of extreme ways. Similar groups of more or less ecstatic mystics and pietists are common in Indian *bhakti*. They also developed in Judaism and Christianity. In the West the classic mystics are solitary and cultivate the experience of "being alone with the Alone," but some of these movements also cultivated such experiences as forms of communion with each other.

Though mosques are not temples, having no shrines, images, or altars, the great mosques of the Orient rival the Holy Kaaba at Mecca as centers of pilgrimage. They are monumental and majestic. They are more than houses of prayer and communion.

Types of Christian Communion

We have already referred to the early Christian communities as being similar in some respects to the Mysteries, in others to covenanted communities, and in still others to wilderness sects. But a more general and enduring trait is their emphasis on the communion of saints and martyrs. Many of the early meetings of Christians took place at the tombs of their dead and their communion meals were in part done in remembrance of Christ and other martyrs. Other meetings were held at night in the homes of members. Anything resembling temple worship was abhorred. Besides the problem of keeping the faith in the face of persecution, the assemblies had to deal with penitents, with infiltration of pagan and Jewish types of piety that were thought to be unChristian, with caring for the poor, and with many ordinary problems of community life under difficult circumstances. In the Eastern churches the use of icons and images in connection with the communion of saints became popular early and increased as the churches grew. The culmination of this type of communion of saints can be seen in the great *iconostat* or screen that encloses the sanctuary of Uspensky Cathedral in Moscow. It contains icons of the four Evangelists, Christ with his Mother, St. John the Baptist, scenes from the life of the Mother of God and of Christ, the major feasts of the Church Calendar, David, Solomon, the Prophets, and the Patriarchs. The aim is to keep this noble company in sight as well as in communion.

Another feature, closely related, of Christian communion is the idea of "The Holy Catholic Church" as "The spiritual body of Christ." Dante expresses this in terms of Scholastic philosophy: "The form of the church is the life of Christ." This means that the spiritual being of Christ on earth is the communion of all the faithful. The visible church is not this Holy Catholic Church which is the invisible form or ideal unity of all saints in all generations. This idea is symbolized in the sacrament of the Eucharist and Holy Communion.

A pluralistic theory of the communion of all the faithful in contrast to the Catholic theory of organic spiritual unity is the Congregationalist Doctrine. According to it, each local congregation of the faithful is in direct covenant relation with God, who is spiritually present in their meetings for worship. In such churches there is a minimum of communion with all the saints, and an emphasis that only saints or the faithful should be members in good standing of a visible congregation. This emphasis is regarded by them as a return to the first and purest generations of Christians.

The most extreme type of individualism in the theory of

communion is found in The Society of Friends (Quakers). Their assemblies are friendly meetings at which each member is supposed to commune individually with the Holy Spirit.

Communions and World Community

The description of types of communion in all religions could be extended indefinitely. But the few types described above may suffice to suggest that there is no universal communion. Mankind cannot be conceived as a single religious community. It takes more than a common Father in Heaven to make all men on earth brothers. As long as mankind lives in a diversity of cultures a general communion is not even a reasonable ideal. The growth of worldwide communication systems, translation systems, and transportation will no doubt promote some kind of world community as well as world conflict. Under these circumstances it is not unreasonable to expect that human beings can gradually learn to understand and respect each other. Even religious bodies and communions, despite their basic differences, can learn to respect each other. They can be good neighbors even if they cannot worship together.

One reason why there is a growing tendency among religions to take each other seriously is because they all have a common enemy. There is a persistent attempt to persuade men that any religion is an illusion and a menace. However, the great majority of unbelievers are skeptical of the value of this campaign against religion in general. It is as reasonable to combat bad religion as it is to combat bad anything. And it is reasonable to believe that there may be some truth in all religions, or at least that no one religion has a monopoly of truth. Even the faithful are becoming more willing to assume that their fidelity to their creed does not imply that all others are false. Fanaticism gives comfort to the common enemy.

This changing attitude is revolutionizing the whole conception of the missionary enterprise. The former ideals of Christians and Muslims that the world is their parish is yielding to the growing dislike of all imperialisms. There are still vestiges of:

"You are doing the Lord's work in your way, and I in His." But missions are less concerned today with aggression and negotiation and competition, and are trying by their interfaith contacts to promote better understanding and respect among religions. They may all agree that "any faith is better than Inter-faith," and that the integrity of each communion is better than an attempt to unite all communions. But they realize that in the growth of worldwide relations, even the religious will be better related. This is not mere toleration but a willingness to accept the relativity of revelations. A revelation must be genuine, but it need not be universal. A religious faith is not like a scientific proposition, either true or false. Fidelity is not a form of knowledge, but of courage, and of love. And religious revelations are food for faith, not information. Religions, like languages, are not easily translated, and never perfectly translatable. Truth can be spoken in any language and believed in any religion. The spirit of religious devotion is perfected rather than corrupted when communicants in one religion understand that there is authenticity in others as well, and that more than one may be genuine.

VII. Sacra, Sacraments, and the Sacred

It has been assumed by certain schools of anthropology and some historians of religion that the most natural and usual occasions for religious rites are the crises of human life: birth, death, adolescence, marriage, victory or defeat, despair or happiness. Celebrations of such occasions are called by the French *rites de passage,* which might be translated freely as "celebrations of turning points in careers." Persons who are strangers to religion and scorn conventional devotions are almost physically forced to turn to religious ceremonies on certain occasions. When a death leads inevitably to a funeral, some kind of appropriate observance is called for. It is true that the available religious services are seldom as appropriate as they should be for funerals, but to have none is certainly inappropriate. Such occasions put religious observances to a severe test, but it is a test that religious bodies should take seriously. In general, there are critical events which obviously call for celebration and more than informal emotional expression. There are times when, to use a biblical expression, it seems that if human beings kept quiet, "the very stones would cry out." To find adequate means of expression, private or public, for such occasions usually requires the skillful combination and cooperation of fine arts. Careful research and experiments in meeting such problems genuinely should be an important part of the professional training of priests and clergy, for they are apt to be asked to officiate. Too often the clergy forget that it is the laymen, the persons in need of a celebration, that their arts should serve. When both laymen and professionals are unprepared for the occasion, the results are pathetic.

In contrast to these celebrations of very special occasions there are attempts to sanctify daily life ceremonially. Judaism, for example, provides formal blessings for practically any act or event of the daily routine. Life may be sacred, but to try to sanctify it continually is ambitious to say the least. However, there are daily occasions that seem to merit daily observance. A decent family meal, served decently and eaten decently merits a decent observance or blessing. Especially, when such meals are getting as rare as such blessings. However, even families and certainly congregations are apt to concentrate their devotions on the extraordinary days. The Seder Feast at Passover and the Fast of the Atonement are central observances in Jewish piety. In general, it is possible to be daily devoted without continual devotions. But there are occasions that naturally call for ritual observance.

A Celebration of Buddha's Birth

Imagine a community of Buddhist monks in their saffron robes assembled in a monastery or *stupa*, surrounded by sacred symbols, carrying monastery gongs, moving in slow procession, chanting to the rhythmic beating of the gongs, the prescribed chapters from their *sutras*. Today is Buddha's birthday, the high point of their religious calendar. They are chanting the following verses from the *Jataka Tales*, the *Nidana-ketha*:

Now when the future Buddha made himself incarnate, the constituent elements of the ten thousand worlds trembled together, quaked, and were shaken violently. The thirty-two good omens showed themselves. Throughout the ten thousand world-systems an immeasurable light shone. The blind received their sight, as if from very longing to behold his glory. The deaf heard noises. The dumb spoke together. The crooked became straight. The lame walked. All prisoners were freed from their fetters. In each hell the fire was extinguished. In the realm of the hungry ghosts hunger and thirst vanished. Wild animals ceased to fear. All illnesses were cured. All men began to speak kindly. Horses neighed and elephants trumpeted gently. Each musical instrument gave forth its note without the hands of a musician. Bracelets and other ornaments jingled of themselves. All the heavens became clear. A cool soft breeze blew pleasantly over all. Rain fell out of season. Underground waters welled up and overflowed.

The birds foresook their flight on high. The rivers stayed their waters' flow. The sea water became sweet. Over all its surface lotuses bloomed of every color. All blossoms bloomed on land and sea. The trunks, branches, and twigs of trees were covered with blossoms. On earth tree-lotuses sprouted by sevens, even splitting rocks. And hanging lotuses bloomed in the sky and rained down everywhere a shower of flowers. In the heavens the gods sang and played. The ten thousand world-systems revolved and crowded together like a bouquet of flowers, a woven wreath of worlds, as fragrant and resplendent as a mass of garlands, or as a sacred altar decked with flowers.

This chant of rejoicing, with its extravagant, exuberant rhetoric, is a kind of praise unfamiliar in the West, where other media are used for expressing supreme joy. Here the whole burden of expressiveness is carried by an uninhibited weaving of a garland of worlds in reverence. To interpret such exaggeration as a faithful record of the miraculous birth of Gautama would be absurd. To regard it as a belief or creed would be scarcely less absurd. It is an inspired libretto for the procession, chanting, and gongs.

Even a Western stranger can share somewhat in the joy and reverence of this celebration. Similarly, a Buddhist may be able to share in the Western celebration of another virgin birth and its way of expressing "great joy unto all peoples." The medieval monks were explicit in making icons of this mystery as a whole, including the angelic music and the lowing of the ox and braying of the ass behind the crib of the Holy Child. Religions have developed their own arts and languages of praise and devotion, and their own cherished calendar of celebrations.

An Early Christian Rite of Initiation Into the Mystery

The two basic sacraments of the Christian communion are baptism and the eucharist. In the massive records that have come down to us from the early Church Fathers there is the following account of the sacrament of baptism as it was celebrated in the year 348 by Bishop Cyril in the Great Basilica of the Resurrection in Jerusalem built by the Emperor Constantine on the traditional site of the Holy Sepulchre. It is the end of the Lenten Season during which the candidates for baptism and initiation into the mystery of communion have been given an intensive course of instruction or catechism by the bishop. The Sacrament of Catechumens for Easter Eve opens:

> Already there is an odor of blessedness upon you, O ye who are soon to be enlightened; already ye are gathering the spiritual flowers to weave heavenly crowns: already the fragrance of the Holy Spirit has breathed upon you: already ye have gathered around the vestibule of the King's palace: may ye be led in also by the King. For blossoms now have appeared upon the trees; may the fruit also be found perfect: Thus far there has been found an inscription of your names, and a call to service, and torches of the bridal train, and a longing for heavenly citizenship.

Before the catechetical lecture by the bishop there is the warning:

> When the lecture is delivered, if a catechuymen ask thee what the teachers have said, tell nothing to him that is without. For we deliver to thee a mystery and a hope of the life to come: Guard the mystery for Him who gives the reward. Let none ever say to thee, "What harm to thee if I also know it?" So too the sick ask for wine; but if it be given at a wrong time, it causes delirium, and two evils arise; the sick man dies and the physician is blamed. Thou art now standing on the border; take heed, pray, to tell nothing out; not that the things spoken are not worthy to be told, but because the ear is unworthy to receive.

When the candidates for baptism are assembled, clothed in white and arranged in rows, a priest lays his hands on the head of each, pronouncing the following exorcism:

> Take notice, Satan, that punishments are threatening you, the day of judgment and of punishment are threatening you, the day that is to come like a burning furnace, in which eternal destruction will come to you and all your angels: Therefore, accursed one, pay honor to the living and true God. Pay honor to Jesus Christ, His Son, and pay honor to the Holy Spirit, in

whose name and power I command you to go out and depart
from this servant of God, whom today the Lord our God Jesus
Christ has deemed worthy to call to His sacred grace, and to
the benediction and water of His baptism, that he may become
His temple through the water of regeneration for the remission
of all sins in the name of our Lord Jesus Christ, who is about
to come.

At the early dawn of Easter, the Bishop addresses the catechumens as follows:

And now, brethren beloved, the word of instruction exhorts
you all to prepare your souls for the reception of the heavenly
gifts. But now the holy day of the Passover is at hand, and ye,
beloved in Christ, are to be enlightened by the Laver of Regeneration. Ye shall therefore again be taught what is requisite,
if God so will; with how great order and devotion ye must enter
in when summoned, for what purpose each of the holy mysteries
of Baptism is performed, and with what reverence and order ye
must go from Baptism to the Holy Altar of God, and enjoy its
spiritual and heavenly mysteries; that your souls being pre-
viously enlightened by the word of doctrine, ye may discover
in each particular the greatness of the gifts bestowed on you by
God.

Then the catechumens are baptized, either by three immersions
or by having water poured over them three times. After which
they pass into the sanctuary. At the door a priest anoints each
head with fragrant oil and recites:

God omnipotent, Father of our Lord Jesus Christ, who has re-
generated you by water and the Holy Spirit, and who has given
unto remission of all your sins Himself, seals you with the chrism
of safety unto life eternal.

At sunrise the neophytes celebrate their first communion, wear-
ing their white gowns. After communion they are blessed by the
bishop and given a drink of honey, water, and milk.

The Eastern Orthodox Churches still close the Easter morning
communion service with the words of St. John Chrysostom, contemporary of Bishops Basil and Cyril, and an author of the
Eastern Liturgy:

Enter ye all into the joy of your Lord; and receive ye your reward, both the first and likewise the second. Ye rich and poor together, hold ye high festival. Ye sober and ye heedless, honor ye the day. Rejoice today, both ye who have fasted and ye who have disregarded the fast. The table is full-laden; feast ye all sumptuously. The calf is fatted; let no one go hungry away. Enjoy ye all the feast of faith; receive ye all the riches of loving-kindness. Let no one bewail his poverty, for the universal kingdom hath been revealed. Let no one weep for his iniquities, for pardon hath shone forth from the grave. Let no one fear death, for the Savior's death has set us free.

The Roman Creeds

While the Greek-speaking Christians in the East were developing these rites of initiation, purification, and resurrection, the Latins were having difficulties in formulating a confession of faith that would unite the local congregations into one, catholic church. During the great persecutions a simple "yes" or "no" might answer the question of who is a Christian and might lead to martyrdom. But by the fourth century the major problems of standardizing a ritual confession arose, partly because there were serious factions in the church, so that a line had to be drawn between orthodox and heretics; partly because converts who were trained in Greek philosophy could not agree on a precise formulation of the doctrine of salvation through Christ. In earlier times, when worship was less formal, it was not necessary to agree on precise doctrines and fixed rituals. For instance, in the second century Justin Martyr described the communion service in this way:

> Bread and wine mixed with water are brought to the bishop, who offers praise and honor to the Father of the Universe through the name of the Son and the Holy Spirit, and gives thanks that God has bestowed these gifts on us, the people responding "Amen." The deacons then distribute to each of those present a portion of the bread and of the wine, and carry portions to absent members of the church.

But by the fifth century it was necessary to include a confession of doctrine as a symbol of unity in communion and devotion. The formula that was then accepted and had been generally used in the sacrament of baptism was known as the Roman Symbol, and is substantially what is now known as the Apostles' Creed. But as the theological and philosophical disputes continued, a series of ecumenical councils was necessary, and under papal insistence a ground for union was finally reached. At the Council of Chalcedon in the year 451 a compromise yielded the following Symbol:

> We, then, following the holy fathers, all with one consent, teach men to confess one and the same Son, our Lord Jesus Christ, the same perfect in Godhead and also perfect in manhood; truly God and truly man, of a reasonable soul and body; consubstantial with the Father according to the Godhead, and consubstantial with us according to the manhood; in all things like us, without sin; begotten before all ages of the Father according to the Godhead, and in these latter days, for us and our salvation, born of the Virgin Mary, the Mother of God, according to the manhood; one and the same Christ, Son, Lord, Only-begotten, in two natures, inconfusedly, unchangeably, indivisibly, inseparably, the distinction of natures being by no means taken away by their union, but rather the property of each nature being preserved, and concurring in one person and one subsistence, not parted or divided into two persons, but one and the same Son and Only-begotten, God the Word, the Lord Jesus Christ.

This agreement led to the adoption of a revision of the Creed that had been adopted at the Council of Nicaea in 325, and this revision is still used as a confession in rituals.

Added to these theoretical differences were devotional conflicts. The Greeks were accustomed to venerating icons. Their altars and sanctuaries, where the eucharist was celebrated, were separated and screened off from the main body of the church and congregation by the *iconostas*, before which lamps were burning as symbols of veneration. The Romans were accustomed to the use of statues. East and West accused each other of idolatry.

The East-West Schism in Christendom

The divergence between the Greek and Roman Churches which culminated in the Schism of 1054 and which is only now being partially healed, was not based on trivialities but on real differences in religious devotion. The reverence for painted icons in the East, following ancient customs, was strengthened by the long conflicts with Islam and Judaism, both of which prohibited images of any kind in protest against idolatry. The Romans too, in their conflict with pagan Rome, had associated the cultus of images with idolatry, and idolatry was abhorred.

In addition, the Eastern Churches had centered their devotions more on the Holy Spirit and the Living Christ, whereas the Western churches glorified Christ on the Cross as Redeemer. The Romans had waged bitter conflicts with Gnostic sects and their theories of sacred wisdom or enlightenment, whereas the Greeks gave increasing emphasis to Santa Sophia. The dedication of the great Cathedral or Basilica of Santa Sophia in Constantinople was interpreted in the West as a challenge. Meanwhile the cult of the Virgin in the Western monasteries was different in spirit from the cult of "The Mother of God" in the East.

The definite split between East and West (which was geographically close to the line that separates East and West today) reflected more than church politics; it was based on deep differences in popular piety and devotions.

The Sacred

Sacred symbols become hallowed even though their meanings undergo radical changes. The important symbols of religious devotion have accumulated a heritage of meaning and become literally meaningful. They are both more sacred and more flexible than doctrines, though doctrines, too, may become largely symbols rather than beliefs. Doctrines must change with changes in knowledge, and these changes may not imply similar changes in faith and devotion. Piety cherishes non-doctrinal symbols because they can give enduring tangible form to a life of devotion that is more enduring in substance than in form or knowledge. The life of faith is not a life of certainty and security, but of commitment and courage. The continuity of form conceals the changes that any kind of vitality is sure to undergo. The crucifix, for instance, has been sacred to Christians for hundreds of eventful years and for many reasons. It supports very different kinds of suffering and salvation, though its primary meaning was martyrdom and it is of intense value and meaning wherever martyrdom is real. But "bearing one's cross" has some kind of significance even when the central tragedy of the Christian gospel and faith have been pushed into the background or even forgotten.

These generalizations might be illustrated by the careers of symbols in other religions as well. For example, there are many Buddhist sects and will be many more. They all seek enlightenment and release from fetters. But even within the Pure Land Schools, which represent escape from the wheel of birth and death as to an unlocated Pure Land, there are many divergent doctrines and techniques for achieving these goals. Nirvana means both fullness and emptiness, both realization and annulment. Some Buddhists merely repeat "Nembutsu" and are saved; others solve riddles. The scope of Buddhist piety, in short, is much greater than any definition of its symbols.

In Islam there has been, ever since the preaching of the Prophet, a great emphasis on the Last Day. It is quite evident that to the Prophet himself this emphasis was an expression of the urgency of reform, the condemnation of current institutions and morals in the sight of an imminent facing of the perfect Judge. But the theory of the Last Day or Day of Judgment is related to the more general respect for a day of doom or end of history, and to a fear of its approach. It serves in general as a powerful sanction for obedience to the Law of Islam and to the moral law, whatever new interpretations of the moral law may be. The more meanings the Last Day has as a symbol, the more revered it becomes.

When such symbols and sacraments remain in the context of lives of devotion, even of very different devotions, they gain in power as particular symbols for human experiences and also as evidence for the meaning of the sacred in general. But when, as also happens, they become detached from real devotions and become sacrosanct, like fetishes that are more than symbols, they can lead to serious delusions and evils. They may become food for philosophers and anthropologists, but their religious life is gone.

VIII. Holy Days and Seasons

ONE of the institutions of a religion is the construction of a calendar of holy days and seasons—times set apart, sacred, consecrated to religious observances and devotions. Religion is, of course, more than devotion to devotions; it is or can be an intrinsic part of the good life; otherwise it is a positive evil. It is good, reasonable, and practical to make provision for regular, periodic celebrations from so-called everyday life, in order to facilitate public as well as private reflection on human life, its history, traditions, institutions, values, and demands. This results in what is known as a religious calendar, composed of stated services, fasts, and feasts. Not all religious observances are solemn, but even when gay and glad they are serious, that is, they are formalities of devotion and reflection, pauses from work, and celebration of stated themes. Theoretically they are privileges, but religious organizations are apt to think of them as obligations of members. When they become merely obligations to organizations, they lose most of their religious value and may even be a positive nuisance. Religious observances are supposed to be good and enjoyable; any organization has a religious as well as a moral responsibility to make them so.

In the background of religious calendars there are mythical structures of human experience and history, sometimes even of a world order. These give structure and meaning not only to the year but to the whole course of human history, from "in the beginning" to "the last day" and even from creation to eternity. The annual calendars provide a wealth of concrete contents for such a general interpretation of the world and history. Every chapter of our survey affords opportunities to refer to these basic ideologies of faith, hope, love, and fear. To recite even the major themes that religions have made out of history, reflection, and imagination would be impossible; and to compare their annual calendars would make of this chapter a bare calendar of calendars. Let us concentrate on one, remembering that there are others.

The universal plot that underlies the Christian calendar was given its classic form by the author of *The Golden Legend,* a book to which we have referred in a preceding chapter. It was composed by St. Jacobus de Voragine (1230-1298), a Dominican monk and Archbishop of Genoa; it has been translated into many vernacular languages and became soon after the invention of printing, a best-seller. It was one of the first books printed by William Caxton, who made substantial revisions for the English edition. The following translation of de Voragine's original *Prologue* will serve to give the general frame for the Church's Calendar:

The whole life of mankind is divided into four periods: the period of wandering; the period of renewal or return into the right way; the period of reconciliation; and the period of pilgrimage.

The period of wandering began with Adam and continued until Moses, for it was Adam who first wandered from the way of God. And this first period is represented in the Church by that part of the year which comes between Septuagint and Easter (Lent). During this part of the year *Genesis* is recited, in which is to be found the account of the first parents' fall.

The period of renewal began with Moses and lasted until the birth of Christ; for it is the period when men were brought by the prophets to the faith and renewed. It is represented in the Church by that part of the year which comes between Advent and Christmas. And during this time *Isaiah* is recited, who treated most clearly of this renewal.

The period of reconciliation is that time when by Christ we were reconciled to God. It is represented in the Church by that part of the year which comes between Easter and Pentecost. And during this time the *Apocalypse* is read, where the mystery of this reconciliation is fully expounded.

Finally the period of pilgrimage is that of our present life, when we stumble like pilgrims over a thousand obstacles. It is represented in the Church by the part of the year between the Octave of Pentecost and Advent. And then there are recited *The*

Books of the Kings, and of *The Maccabbees,* where numerous conflicts are described, symbolizing the spiritual warfare which is inflicted upon us.

As to the section of the year which comes between Christmas and Septuagint, it belongs partly to the period of reconciliation (from Christmas to the Octave of Epiphany) and partly to the period of pilgrimage (from Octave of Epiphany to Septuagint).

But in spite of the fact that the period of wandering preceded that of renewal, the Church prefers to begin its year with the time of renewal, that is, with Advent; and that for two reasons: (1) because of the mere fact that it is the time of renewal, when the Church renews all of its offices; (2) because, by beginning with the period of wandering, the Church would seem to begin with error. And that is why it is not proper to follow the order of time, just as the Evangelists frequently did not follow it in their accounts of the life of the Lord.

Advent, or the coming of the Lord, is celebrated during four weeks, to signify that this coming is in four different senses: in the flesh, in the spirit, in death, and at the Last Judgment. The last week remains incompleted, to signify that the glory of the elect, which will be given to them at the last coming of the Lord, will be without end. But though the fast of Advent is in reality fourfold, the Church is principally concerned with but two of its forms, namely, the advent in the flesh and the advent at the Last Judgment. And accordingly the fast of Advent is in part a fast of rejoicing, in part a fast of contrition.

No comment is needed on this eloquent *Prologue.* It provides the theoretical outline for the Christian faith as well as for the Church's Calendar. As a matter of history, however, it is worth noting how this calendar gradually took shape. It is also worth knowing what other factors contributed to this shape in addition to this philosophy of history.

Christmas, to begin with, both in its time of year and manner of celebration was related to other celebrations at the time of the winter solstice. There were festivals devoted primarily to rejoicing at the return of longer days, more light, and the advent of springtime. The Jewish Feast of Lights (*Hanukkah*) is related to both Christmas and Epiphany (January 6, Twelfth Night). It was on this latter date that the early Christians celebrated the Nativity before this feast was moved ahead to December 25.

The Mithraic Festival, especially popular among Roman soldiers, was held on December 25. In Rome, *La Befana,* the witch, still brings gifts to good children and coals to the bad on Twelfth Night. In Russia St. Nicholas brought gifts. Yule time, in pre-Christian Britain was a feast of home, hearth, and hospitality. During the Middle Ages, as the Church began to revere the Holy Family, the custom grew of setting up pottery figurines representing the scene of the Nativity, usually including the three Kings, though they were supposed to have come later to adore the Child.

New Year's was excluded from the religious calendar because the beginning of the secular Roman year had no Christian significance (though it was related to the pagan Roman Calendar). But gradually the churches were forced by popular demand to provide observances on what came to be called Watch Night or Sylvester Eve. In pagan Rome and secular life in Europe the New Year was celebrated by merriment; but when the Church included New Year's Day in its calendar, it was as a day of penitence, meditation, and resolution (especially after Sylvester Eve).

The Lenten Season had been in pagan Rome and Greece a time for purification rites, prayers for good crops, and memorials for the dead. The Jews celebrated a pre-Passover fast.

The joyous festival of Easter is so named after an Anglo-Saxon goddess of spring. The early Christians connected it with Passover. Pentecost is related to the Jewish agricultural Festival of Weeks (fifty days). At that time the Christians celebrated it as the descent of the Holy Spirit on the Disciples; after the thirteenth century it came to be known as Trinity Sunday.

The fast of human pilgrimage during the summer months, so eloquently defined by Voragine, was appropriately observed by nonobservance. Later the "dead" season was interrupted by the addition of the Feast of Corpus Christi in June, and of the Assumption of the Virgin in mid-August. These dates, too, were related to secular celebrations.

To the growing power and popularity of the cult of the Virgin the Calendar owes a number of important holy days. The

Annunciation (Lady Day) on March 25 began to be celebrated as early as the seventh century. The Immaculate Conception of the Virgin (by her mother), December 5, has been celebrated since the ninth century, but neither the days nor the doctrines were officially recognized until 1477 and were not fully sanctioned until 1854. The Assumption of the Virgin and her Coronation, August 15, though celebrated throughout the Middle Ages, and glorified by the painters of the Renaissance, was not accepted until very recently as a dogma of the Church. The Nativity of the Virgin is celebrated on September 6, and her Purification on February 2.

During feudal times the calendar became so full of holy days that were celebrated as holidays that finally the governments and middle classes, alarmed because there were not enough days for the harvest and other agricultural labor, placed restrictions on the number of holy holidays.

The Sabbath is the basic holy day of the whole Calendar not only for all Christians, but also for Jews (Saturday) and Muslims (Friday). The early Christians still celebrated the Jewish Sabbath until the Emperor Constantine in the year 381 shifted the Christian Sabbath to "the venerable Day of the Sun." Some churches still celebrate the seventh day rather than Sunday. In all three religions, the Sabbath is consecrated as a day of rest from labor and as a day for public worship. It has been honored conscientiously by the secular authorities.

However, recent transformations and transportations in both urban and rural life are seriously threatening the holiness of Sunday or Saturday and are substituting a long week-end with secular types of recreation, including "drive-in worship." Not only the Sabbath but the whole religious calendar is continuing to adapt itself to changes in modern cultures. But this process of adaptation is slow and difficult, as the account of the Calendar's history from the beginning illustrates. Hallowed institutions are by their nature the least yielding. But the probabilities are that there will continue to be a religious calendar, though the dates, names, and modes of celebration will change. It is not impossible that what now are twenty-four hour general strikes may acquire a religious status.

The inclusion of Thanksgiving Day in the religious and secular calendars of the United States is one illustration of such adaptation. But what is a more serious problem and a real uncertainty is what the future may bring from the growing competition between religious and secular arts of celebration.

In the times when religious institutions were wealthy and could count on the cooperation of the arts they created masterpieces of the arts which added esthetic delight to sacred devotions. It is still possible, for example, to witness a pontifical high mass in the Church of St. Francis of Assisi at Assisi, with the sublime music of Palestrina and Pergolesi, elegant pageantry and illumination, frescoes by Giotto on the walls, concluded by a magnificent procession. All of this is just the opposite of what Saint Francis was devoted to, but it shows that the glorification of God by the Church can be done in a way that is glorious from a human standpoint. The triumphs of religious art and celebration are still conspicuous, and many of them are quite modern. But these great achievements of religious art are surrounded by the tawdriness, vacuity, and fanaticism of the public performances of religious devotions. When formalities become regular public functions in a civilized society, religious bodies owe it to themselves, to their Lord, and to civilization to be worthy of this cultural environment and to make their contributions as best they can to the arts and to public decency.

IX. Religious Bodies and Social Services

Institutional Religion

LIKE the secular arts, religion, if it is to make a significant contribution to civilized life, must be more or less institutionalized. It is never merely an institution, for in both the most primitive and the most advanced cultures religion is also a private, personal and unconventional form of experience. A *shaman* is recognized among his primitive tribal fellows as a person with peculiar endowments and special powers; and though, like a family physician, he must know the standardized arts of healing, he acts professionally as an individual and may employ devices of his own invention. In all ages and cultures there are charismatic persons (prophets, mystics, religious innovators) who depart from sacred traditions under the impact of a personal revelation. However, religious institutions have a remarkable talent for assimilating rebels and for putting a halo on a visionary who, during his lifetime may have had a stormy, alienated career, despised or persecuted by his contemporaries. Religions share with the arts and sciences in having a fringe of individual variation and rebellion despite their established, institutional norms and ways. On the whole, religions are apt to be less organized than the sciences and technologies, but more than the fine arts.

Being a form of devotion and piety, a religion is apt to be bound more intimately to its past and to hallowed conventions than are the arts and sciences. It naturally aims to be conservative, but it is not naturally reactionary. The venerable is its specialty, but it may be prophetic in its devotion rather than traditional.

As social organizations, religious bodies are of two kinds: those that are politically established and supported as a public utility, and those that are supported voluntarily by their members. No religion is bound to adhere permanently to either kind. There are Christian churches of each kind. In Pakistan and Indonesia, where Islam is not indigenous, there is an attempt to create an Islamic establishment. Similarly among the Buddhists of Ceylon and Burma. Hinduism, Taoism, Confucianism, and Shintoism are notably traditional but have a very loose and minimal organization. Buddhism is theoretically less traditional but is still becoming increasingly organized. Statisticians refer to all these as religious bodies and attempt to measure their memberships; but both the quantity and quality of membership are so indefinite for many of these "bodies" that the statistics mean little.

Though state churches and other establishments of religion are distinguished legally from voluntary or free religious organizations (which are often referred to by the established as "sects," the line between religious services and social services is by no means well defined. With few exceptions, religious bodies and their services are treated as public and benevolent organizations; their activities, like those of schools, hospitals, arts, sciences, and sports, are regarded as significant contributions to civilized society regardless of the methods by which they are financed. However, the religious institutions usually regard themselves as much more important or basic than they really are, and are therefore apt to be on the defensive in their relations with other institutions. The contrast between spiritual and temporal powers and authorities with which Western peoples have become familiar through centuries of conflict, is not recognized in the majority of other cultures. In modern Israel there is an insistence on the separation of the spiritual and temporal authorities (imported from Europe and America), despite the small minority which defends the ancient unity of the secular and the sacred law. The same is true of the Muslims in Turkey. But among the Arabs this attitude is regarded as a form of infidelity.

Administration

Religious institutions, like secular, vary in degree of centralized government. In Judaism, human authority (under God) is very democratic and local. Local congregations are organized as independent bodies, though the congregations are loosely associated. Their rabbis or teachers do not govern; neither do their priests. In Christianity there can be found all conceivable types of church government from anarchy to rigid hierarchy. No church has ever been literally "catholic" or universal in its jurisdiction. Roman Catholic, Greek Catholic, and Anglo-Catholic are all contradictions-in-terms if taken as institutions or governments. Protestantism has never been unified as an institution or even as a single movement. Until recently, almost all the churches have tried to defend themselves against heresy, but today heresy cannot be legally defined, for it is impossible to fix definitely the boundaries and formulas of Christian doctrine. Ever since the founding of the Christian church bishops have exercised an impressive degree of authority and have promoted law and order among the clergy. But by far the most influential factor in Christian institutions has been the parish priest or local pastor. The cooperation of the lay members and the clergy in any local congregation is the basic strength of Christianity as an institution.

The Laity

Recognition of the rights and leadership of lay members of the churches is a relatively recent development. Even the Independents and Dissenters of the seventeenth century, with the exception of a few democratic groups who repudiated the clergy entirely, like the Society of Friends, recognized the leadership of the clergy. But increasingly pastors or teachers were being selected by the laity, even when the clergy were still ordained by higher authority. The rise of lay leadership is mainly a twentieth century trend, and still exists on paper more than in fact. However, new ideas in the realm of doctrine as well as in the realm of social services are being sponsored by laymen (as well as by the clergy) in both the Catholic and Protestant churches.

Along with the growth of lay initiative there is a growing

secularization in the activities of both laymen and clergy. Even the churches that are most committed to the separation of church and state are emphasizing the intimate relations between ecclesiastical and secular interests and obligations. The so-called "fundamentalist" conception that the salvation of the soul is radically separated from the welfare of mind and body in society is rapidly losing ground.

The Social Gospel

Religious trends such as these in the Christian churches are conspicuous in all religions and cultures; they have been stimulated more by the increased contacts between religious and other institutions than by changes in doctrine or formal faith. Changes have followed sometimes reluctantly and gradually those that have developed in human devotions generally. The secularization of religious devotion became urgent as new forms of civil and social services were demanded of congregations. The pressing need for schools, hospitals, and relief of poverty had been recognized and to some extent met during the nineteenth century, but the present revolutionary needs for peace, counseling, recreation, better economic and race relations, and promotion of welfare reforms generally have been felt by religious as by all institutions and have called for action and commitment. The result has been a general breakdown of the traditional distinctions between the material and the spiritual, the temporal and the eternal, the practical and the devotional. Traditional forms and concepts of religious devotion have not been abandoned, but are constantly being reinterpreted. The concepts of heaven and hell, sin and salvation, divine judgment and human depravity, charity and righteousness, atonement and mercy, are all being applied to the urgent problems of life here and now. Religious institutions in all cultures are adapting themselves and their ideas to the new environment and its problems. Escape mechanisms are giving way to sharing in the concerns of other institutions. Examples of this new orientation could be given from all the so-called "living faiths of mankind." Here are a few typical expressions taken from recent Christian literature and declarations:

1. From a sermon by a Protestant clergyman, 1897:

> Infallible authority is undesirable. God has not given it to his children. He has given them something far better,—life. There is as little a short and easy way to truth as to virtue. It is given to us not to save us from struggle, and growth by struggle, but to inspire us to struggle that we may grow. God is from eternity the Life-Giver and giving life costs God something; that is the secret of growth in the impartation of life. This is what the Bible means by what we call vicarious sacrifice. The great laws of life which natural science has elucidated are analogous to, if not identical with, the laws of spiritual life. The latter are to be interpreted by the former. (Lyman Abbott)

2. From a sermon by a Protestant clergyman, 1904:

> The people have outrun the preacher and the church. Strong spiritual movements lay hold of the masses sooner than upon those who live and think among established theories. The spirit is a wind that blows freest in the open. Consequently there are today movements going on in the churches of which they are only half aware or treat but slightingly. One must think twice before one speaks lightly of such lay bodies. No matter how crude or trifling they may appear, nor what mistakes they make, they cannot make more or worse than the churches from which they sprang. With the instinct of young life, they look to life for a field of action. (Theodore T. Munger)

3. From the "Creed" of a Catholic layman, 1927:

> I believe that no tribunal of any church has any power to make any decree of any force in the law of the land, other than to establish the status of its own communicants within its own church. I believe in the support of the public school as one of the cornerstones of American liberty. I believe in the right of every parent to choose whether his child shall be educated in a public school or in a religious school. I believe in the principle of noninterference by this country in the internal affairs of other nations, and that one should stand steadfastly against such interference by whomsoever it may be urged. And I believe in the common brotherhood of man under the common fatherhood of God. (Alfred E. Smith)

4. Some Ideals of the Federal Council of Churches, 1932:

Application of the Christian principle of redemption to the treatment of offenders; reform of penal and correctional methods and institutions, and of criminal court procedure.

Justice, opportunity and equal rights for all, mutual goodwill and cooperation among racial, economic, and religious groups.

Repudiation of war, drastic reduction of armaments, participation in international agencies for the peaceable settlement of all controversies; the building of a cooperative world order.

Recognition and maintenance of the rights and responsibilities of free speech, free assembly, and a free press, the free encouragement of mind with mind as essential to the discovery of truth.

5. Some Principles of Catholic Social Action, 1948:

Christian social principals, rooted in the moral law, call insistently for cooperation not conflict, for freedom not repression, in the development of economic activity. Cooperation must be organized —organized for the common good; freedom must be ordered— ordered for the common good.

6. Rethinking Missions, 1932:

We must be willing to cooperate with non-Christian agencies for social improvements; and to foster the initiative of the Orient in defining the ways in which we shall be invited to help.

We desire to use the privilege of laymen in avoiding as far as possible the language of the unexplained symbol. We believe it to be one of the necessities of the present hour that Christianity should be able to make more immediate connection with common experience and thought. Especially in addressing the Orient it is imperative that we present our faith in terms which those wholly unfamiliar with the history of Christian doctrine can understand. (Laymen's Foreign Mission Inquiry Report)

7. From a book by a Protestant Clergyman, 1940:

From now on, religion becomes a conscious and purposeful direction of the spiritual life of man toward the fuller realization of the human values potential in a scientific and democratic culture. That such a perspective involves a Copernican revolution in institutional religion is fully granted. However, that this out-

look and the religious reconstruction which it involves is a "break" with the deeper life of religion is rejected. To awaken man's spiritual nature in such a quest is both revelation and inspiration.
(Floyd S. Kenney)

Such preaching is now common in Christian pulpits, though not general. Similar ideas are being presented in other religions.

Public Piety and Religious Movements

It is now a truism to say that mankind is living through a revolutionary period, and it should be common knowledge that religion is sharing in this revolution.

The institutional status of religion may be undergoing radical changes which yet cannot be clearly perceived. New religions will arise as they always have. This is especially true in Eastern cultures where modern movements are taking shape. For example, in Japan the traditional Shinto rites are continuing to be performed as expressions of public piety. But increasing religious importance is being given to voluntary religious sects and organizations which are not traditional.

What the future for religious institutions will bring to communist countries is difficult to imagine. It is quite certain that attempts to liquidate the traditional devotions in communist Russia and China, have been given up as impractical and unnecessary. As public piety takes more political forms, religious devotions may become less institutionalized. In time, political faiths may generate religious institutions, which will consecrate what is now revolutionary. But this whole matter is very speculative. It is arbitrary to conceive today's ideological faiths as religions merely because problems of orthodoxy are arising and intense devotion is becoming critical. For both devotions and orthodoxy have long standing political histories and secular literature. But it is possible that the ideological devotions may acquire more religious forms in the future.

This whole situation illustrates the difficulty in drawing a sharp distinction between organized civil services (whether public or private) and religious institutions. What the future institutions will be cannot be foretold either as to new kinds of devotion or religious traditions. But it is quite shortsighted and contrary to the history of human civilization to assume that religion has no future. Though the future existence of some of our present religious institutions is problematical, these are not apt to yield except under pressure from new religious institutions with more vitality. Religious life has proven to be tougher to uproot than its enemies have supposed; like all life, it has a way of sprouting anew. This is not life eternal, but it is genuine regeneration.

X. Divine Beings

The Divine

BOTH the real world and the world of the imagination are full of wonderful beings. And wonder itself is among them. It lives between the real and the imagined and continually gets them so mixed up that it is difficult to pull them apart. Children can raise more questions than adults can answer, but adults too have unanswerable questions. Human beings of all ages have faced the wonderful, and whether existence is now more wonderful or less so than it was (or is) to the ignorant is one of those questions best left unanswered. The term wonder in this chapter serves as a convenient symbol for the fact that the objects to which human beings address themselves in religious, as in daily life, are a mixture of things believed, unknown, feared, admired, loved, enjoyed, or simply accepted as familiar. Beliefs are always involved with other attitudes, emotional and reflective, so that it is difficult to tell clearly to what or to whom a religious rite or devotion is addressed.

When a being is regarded as divine, it is never quite clear what divine means. But for our purposes in this chapter it is convenient to use the term vaguely to mean the being or beings to which any religious act is addressed. A religious person seldom can give any precise explanation of such a being, and about all we can do here is to indicate the great diversity that exists in different religions and even within the same religion. There have been many attempts to discover the origin of such beings and to describe their history or revolution. Instead of commenting on these attempts, which have been inconclusive, we might as well face the diversity itself, and consider some of these beings, some that are addressed religiously now, and some that have been so addressed in the past and are now forgotten.

Heaven and Earth

Long before there were any attempts to rationalize piety, and to make a theology of its objects, there were pious references to Heaven and the mandates of Heaven. In many cultures the idea of the realm of the stars is very vague. Heaven is sometimes conceived as being beyond the dome or vault of the sky and stars, but usually the location of heaven is not a serious religious concern. Many primitive people refer to sky-spirits or to the Great Spirit of the Sky but pay them no devotions, since these spirits are too remote to care. But in China and Japan Heaven has a basic religious meaning rather than an astronomical orientation. Those men who know the Heavenly Principles are sages, and men are called sons of Heaven. The most common mandates of Heaven are sunshine and rain, right and wrong. Wisdom, law, power, masculine and feminine are all based on Heavenly mandates.

The ancient scriptures of Japan and of Shinto (the way of the gods) begin about as follows (there are minor variations in the texts):

> Of old, when heaven and earth were not yet separated and the feminine and masculine principles had not yet been distinguished, there was a chaos like an egg, and in this chaos there was a living germ. . . . The clear and pure part spread out thin and became the heavens; the heavy and dark part became the earth. . . . Hereupon sacred beings were generated between heaven and earth. . . . Now a thing appeared between heaven and earth like a reed stalk. Hereupon it changed itself into a god.

On the high plain of Heaven there reigned the Divine Master of the High Center of Heaven, who had many gods under him. But religious myth begins not up on the high plain but when, after a series of such appearances of single reed stalks, there arose "above the slime" a *pair* of deities who were commanded to "make, consolidate, and give birth to this drifting land." The story of this Pair, Izanagi and Izanami, of their creation of the islands of Japan, of the Sun-goddess (Amaterasu), of the Storm-god, the Fire-god, and others, is one of the most charming of classic myths. The Temple of the Sun-goddess at Ise is the holy-of-holies of the Imperial cultus and of popular devotions and pilgrimages.

In China no such mythology developed. Confucianism and the more ancient Taoism, base their principles on the Heavenly Way or the Way of Nature, the true way (*tao*) of all ways.

Pantheons

The ancient scriptures of India, however, the *Vedas*, give a detailed account of an ordered system of divine beings, the *Devas* or shining ones. According to one of the accepted traditions, there are thirty-three Devas, assigned by elevens to three realms: the realm of light, where *Dyaus-Pitar* (father sky), *Ushas* (dawn), *Surya* (sun), *Varuna* (heavenly order) and others are located; the middle air where *Indra* (thunder), *Rudra* (storm), *Vayu* (wind), and others hold sway; and the lower air where *Agni* (fire), *Soma* (sacred libation), *Prthivi* (mother earth) and others are to be found.

In the *Zend Avesta*, the sacred scriptures of the Zoroastrians, the Indo-Iranian pantheon is reduced from its galaxy of nature powers to two powers, and these are moralized more definitely than in the *Rig Veda*. *Ahura Mazda* is praised as Lord of the High Realm of Light, but light becomes the symbol of wisdom; hence, in the *gathas* (hymns) of Zarathustra (Zoroaster) the Prophet, *Ahura Mazda* is Lord of Wisdom. Gradually in the development of Zoroastrian doctrine, Lord is interpreted as moral power and the original pantheon becomes practically an ethical monotheism. In opposition to this power of Light and Wisdom is the dark power of the Deceiver, *Angra Mainyu,* Power of Evil; but this power is not divine and the struggle between the two powers is temporal and will end in the victory of the Lord of Light. In the cultus, fire is a sacred element, symbol of Ahura Mazda. The *devas,* who were originally the servants of Ahura Mazda, become his attributes or essences: the Holy Spirit of Truth, Right Order and Law, General Benevolence, Devotion, Integrity, and Immortality.

The Olympian pantheon of ancient Greek gods, supplemented by the gods of Earth below, should not need a detailed introduction. Suffice it to note that this pantheon is of a different type. The Vedic gods represented natural beings and their natural functions; the Zoroastrian pantheon represented a moral hierarchy. The Greek gods, however, formed a genuine community, analogous to human society; they personified and represented the various traits of human character and social relations. Thus, in addition to being powers, they became the prototypes of human virtues and vices.

The Buddhist hierarchy of divine beings is unique and complicated, for there are several types of Buddhas. Gautama Buddha, like Confucius, repudiated all the traditional divinities as well as the doctrine of a soul subject to reincarnation. He retained only the doctrine of *karma* or the universal moral law, and reinterpreted the wheel of birth and death as the constant new births that take place with the ever-turning wheel of the law. He wished to free his middle way from entanglement in any of the traditional cults. Accordingly, many of the most rigid (*Hinayana*) followers prefer not to regard Buddhism as a religion at all. (This is true of the Confucianists as well.) However, Buddhism soon developed not only its monasteries but many of the traits of the religions in the countries to which it spread. Meanwhile Gautama Buddha was himself made a sacred being in Hinduism; he was recognized as one of the ten incarnations of Vishnu. Buddhism gradually adopted three types of Buddhas, none of them called gods, but otherwise venerated as though they were the gods. There are: First, human buddhas, enlightened human beings who experienced *nirvana* and escaped from the wheel of birth and death. Then, there are *Bodhisattvas*, enlightened human beings who had been freed from the wheel and could have entered *nirvana,* but chose to tarry among human beings as saviors and guides. Lastly, there are *Dhyani* buddhas, who are not earthly beings, but buddhas of contemplation, lords of paradise or representatives of the absolute, eternal buddha-essence. The spiritual realms of these buddhas received popular adoration as land of bliss, western paradise or pure land.

The Buddhists of Nepal and Tibet worshipped a pantheon of heavenly buddhas and bodhisattvas, but also took over from Hinduism the idea that each heavenly being has its divine counterpart or consort. In the Tibetan monasteries or lamaseries there was a group of thirty-five buddhas to whom the monk made ritual confessions. There were also many demons, guardian spirits, and other features of the primitive cults in those areas, which Buddhism there incorporated.

Trinities

A common form of Buddhist shrine is a grouping of three divine beings. The most usual of such trinities is: In the center a *Dhyani* or heavenly buddha of contemplation; on his right, Gautama Buddha, and on his left, a *Bodhisattva* (in China, usually *Kuanyin*). The most popular of the heavenly buddhas is Amitabha (Amida), the Lord of Paradise. Kuan Yin (Kwannon) in China and Japan was a goddess of mercy and protector of children before she was adopted as the female form of the Indian bodhisattva, *Avalokiteshvara*. A prominent member of a trinity is also *Maitreya*, the buddha who will usher in the next era, or world cycle, successor to Gautama. *Manjursi*, Buddha of Transcendent Wisdom and Guardian of the Law, is also a popular member of trinities.

In Hinduism the most important trinity is represented by the *Trimurti* (three faces of) *Siva* as creator, preserver, and destroyer. Another traditional trinity is the triad of Brahma (creator), *Vishnu* (preserver), and *Siva* in the form of the female demon, *Durga* (destroyer).

These trinities are groups of divine beings assembled for devotions. They are not in idea like the Christian Trinity, a single God in three manifestations.

XI. Monotheism and Humanism

THERE are two ways of interpreting the objects of devotion and two types of systematic theology: One, which was the concern of the preceding chapter, is the ideology of a particular faith. It includes the identification and systematization of gods who have proper names, such as Vishnu, Zeus, Yahweh. The other type is not related exclusively to any particular religion or institution. In the secular context of humanistic studies and metaphysics "God" is a term used for the universal ground of being. We are not concerned here with this secular theology or philosophy, which seeks to avoid being an ideology. In the medieval system of Scholasticism theology was called the queen of the sciences and was supposed to have been founded by Aristotle. This was an illusion.

But there is a type of religious theology that tries to reconcile these two ways of conceiving a deity. It regards God as a universal object of a universalized piety. God in this sense is not a proper name, nor does it imply individuality. God is not a jealous god, not a god among gods or the object of a particular tradition or institution. God would be the object of a devotion that is universal. A universal religion would not be a particular religion that had crowded out all others; nor would its god be the god of the whole of humanity. It would be universal not in a geographical or historical sense, but in a logical sense. God as universal would be the ultimate object of any religion if it were devoted to universality. God would then be a concrete universal, not an abstraction: God might be The Truth but not the idea of truth; he might be Love, but not the essence of love. The knowledge of such a divine being is what modern monotheism is trying to explore. Theologians exploring this theory try to free themselves from any actual, institutionalized religion, but not from religion in general. They believe that the great religions are attempting in their particular idioms to express a universal piety or devotion, and that it is this universal element in actual religions that enables them to tolerate each other. Such theology attempts to reveal the true god of any good religion, and in this sense to be responsible to God, not to any particular religion. Now and then a minor prophet in his enthusiasm will exclaim: "God hates religion; all He wants is fidelity." These critical theologians are apt to be suspicious of any institutionalized channel of Grace, of arbitrary forms of devotion, and of special revelations. Their kind of piety is a radical departure from traditional forms, but it has serious difficulty in making itself genuinely universal.

The Cosmos

There has been since ancient times a devotion to The-One-and-All, which takes on different forms and names, but which is a kind of universal ideology. The ancient Stoics cultivated it; it was associated with Cosmopolitanism: it sometimes called itself Pantheism; and during the period of The Enlightenment was called Natural Religion. A few classic expressions of this faith must suffice, for it is difficult to make a systematic formulation of it.

When, in Euripides' *The Trojan Women,* Hecuba realizes the doom of Troy and her own doom, she utters her famous prayer:

> O Thou base of earth and also King,
> Whoe'er Thou be, unfathomable,
> Zeus, natural necessity or mortal mind,
> To Thee I pray; for silently thy steps
> Lead all things mortal to judgment,

Then she follows this expression of faith in universal judgment with a cry of despair over all human faiths:

> In vain we sacrificed. Had but the gods
> Not cast us thus beneath the earth,
> We should have gone down unrenowned. . . .
> Tis the living that value such vanities.

Euripides saw the twilight of the patron deities of Athens as well as of Troy. This prayer reflects more than a failure of nerve; it was the end of history. Greece was going down into the history of human vanities. But this history was a chapter in the universal administration.

The Stoic Roman Emperor, Marcus Aurelius, (121-180 A.D.) wrote in Greek his meditations, *To Myself;* from these golden sayings a few paragraphs will illustrate his type of piety:

> As you arise mornings, say to yourself: today I shall meet busybodies, arrogant, deceitful, envious, unsocial persons. . . . I who have seen that they are akin to me by blood and seed, partake with me in intelligence and sacredness cannot be injured by them, nor can I hate my kin. For we are all made for cooperation—like two hands, feet, eyelids, or rows of teeth. To rebel against each other is therefore contrary to our nature. . . . Say to yourself: I am an experienced old man, not a slave, nor a puppet pulled by strings to make unsocial gestures. I can cease being discontented with the present, and need not fear the future. . . . What the gods give is all providence. . . . What is good for the cosmos is good for each of its parts and maintains it. . . . Let these principles be enough for you and live by them. Quit thirsting for books, so that you can die without regrets, cheerfully, sincerely thanking the gods. . . .
>
> A man's soul does itself violence when it becomes a kind of boil or tumor on the universe . . . or when it is overwhelmed by pleasure or pain . . . or when it acts without aim or thought. . . . For the goal of a rational animal is to follow reason, the law and policy of the cosmos, which is the oldest community.

Such piety found classic expression in modern times as well. One of them is in the ideal of the intellectual love of God as expressed in the *Ethics* of Baruch de Spinoza (1632-77):

> The wise man . . . is scarcely at all disturbed in mind, but, being conscious of himself, and of God, and of things by a certain eternal necessity . . . always possesses true acquiescence of spirit.

Our God Is One Lord

There is an emergence of such piety and of a theology to express it within historical religions. But the conception of the universal administration of God is related less to the concept of a cosmos or natural order, more to the course of human history. This idea is present in the ancient *Upanishads* of the Brahmans, and it has become the basic idea of the Vedanta school of philosophy and religion in India. Here the distinction is between the Vedic god, *Brahma* and the Absolute, *brahma* or *brahm,* One-Without-a-Second, *Advaita* (non-dual). This universal reality is the source of all beings, and the receptacle into which all beings return, like individual rivers into the Ocean of Being. There are expressions akin to this in the Hymns of Zarathustra, which are basic to the monotheistic trends in Zoroastrian and Manichaean religion.

Also preached by some of the Prophets of Israel was a universal administration of God over all peoples. The rabbis of Judaism have developed this interpretation of the sacred *Shemah:* Hear, O Israel, the Lord our God is One Lord. This is interpreted to mean that the One Lord is King of the Universe, who rules the affairs of all mankind and not only those of his chosen people.

In Islam, too, though the faithful call upon God as *Allah,* this is not a proper name for the god of Islam, but simply the way Islam refers to the universal Lord. This idea is also found in the hymns of the Indian poet Shankara, the authentic prophet of *Advaita,* and in the poems of Kabir, who unites the monisms of Hinduism and Islam.

In the present world situation, the World Council of Christian Churches in 1958 gave expression to this faith as follows:

> In the present age man's conception of the classical religions is undergoing considerable if not radical change. . . . In part it is due to the realization that religion in its traditional form is being challenged by modern civilization and is in danger of being outmoded, and to a desire to preserve and reinterpret those beliefs and values which are claimed as abiding and are considered to be the only hope of saving the world from swift and final disintegration and destruction.
>
> In their renewed form many religions claim a world mission which is being pursued with vigor, particularly in the West.
>
> It is these "living faiths" in this new situation which must be

studied and it is to man living in these faiths that the word of God must be addressed.

(Division of Studies of the World Council of Churches, Bulletin, Vol. IV, No. 1, April 1958)

These theologians and religious leaders wish to make it very clear that the living faiths of today are not to be confused with the natural religion of the Enlightenment. The classic formulation in Alexander Pope's lines:

> Father of all in ev'ry age
> In ev'ry clime adored,
> By saint, by savage, and by sage,
> Jehovah, Jove, or Lord.

assumes the religious identity, or at least equivalance, of all faiths. No such universality is asserted by contemporary monotheism. The search for the Universal God springs not from the unity of all religions or from nature or from reason, but from man's need for a common piety in a particular crisis.

Humanistic Devotion

Theological monotheism among religions is a counterpart to the non-theological, humanistic interpretation of living faiths and its plea for a more morally general union of mankind. The contemporary humanist movement is not interested in uniting the living faiths religiously, but in getting their support for a general recognition of common human needs and ideals for peace, justice, and happiness. The aim is to unite devotion of all men to each other and to interpret their fidelity to their God in these terms. The humanists seek to get men to accept the idea that God is essentially of and for men, and that particular revelations if they have genuine human value should be interpreted as human responses in human crises. Humanists do not believe in worshipping men or mankind, but neither will they bow to a Perfect Being or to any theism. Devotion to perfection should mean human perfection and should be worked out as a human responsibility. A good formulation of this attitude and of the particular context in which it is needed was given by Dag Hammarskjold in 1957, when as Secretary General of the United Nations he dedicated a room for meditation in the Headquarters Building:

> This house must have one room, one place which is dedicated to silence, dedicated to silence in the outward sense and stillness in the inner sense. . . . Its altar is an empty altar, empty not because there is no God, but empty because God is worshipped in so many forms. . . . We want to bring back the idea of worship, devotion to something which is greater and higher than ourselves. . . . We want to bring to everybody's mind the fact that every single one of us is faced, in his handling of the heritage of the riches of this earth, with the choice between the ploughshare and the sword.
>
> . . . There are many other opportunities for devout men to cooperate in considering ways and means for preserving the rights of freedom of faith; to evaluate human achievements and world affairs in the light of ethical and spiritual teachings which have been the guideposts of human association through the ages; to enlarge our horizons and inspire us with a vision that may give direction and meaning to the future of civilization and mankind as a whole.

The line between the monotheistic theologians and the nontheistic humanists is not as sharp as doctrinal strife makes it appear. Both are critical of the attitudes of traditional religions and doctrines, but when both become doctrinaire in turn there is danger that they may merely add to the number of sects. For doctrinal differences often obscure instead of clarifying whatever universal elements there are in devotion, and they bring upon themselves the reproaches of other preachers in the regular pulpits. Humanist religion is most useful and constructive not as a separate religious organization, but as an enlightenment within religious bodies. There have been humanist popes and bishops and there may well be more. "A new Renaissance must come," wrote Albert Schweitzer, "much greater than the Renaissance in which we stepped out of the Middle Ages, the great renaissance in which the whole of mankind is discovered." Religious ideas of this kind seem to be gaining ground and to point less to the formation of a universal religion or theology than to a greater understanding among existing religions.

There are theologians who claim that religions must sacrifice themselves to God, and there are humanists who wish the death of gods. But such drastic measures seem uncalled for so long as there are living faiths. In any case, religions are not apt to sacrifice themselves to theology or humanism; and if they sacrifice themselves to God, new faith will rise.

XII. Faith and Fidelity

"BEING devoted to" implies "believing in." To believe in something or somebody is an attitude of trust. The relation of this attitude to other attitudes takes us into the heart of the psychology of religion. The psychology of religion is past its infancy, but it has attracted psychologists whose primary interest is pathology and who suffer from the naive prejudice that all religious experience is abnormal. They promptly find it full of infantilism, illusion, fantasy, obsession, and escape mechanisms. To be sure, religious pathology is a fertile field for psychiatry and it is well to have medical specialists who can deal with religious insanity. Religious diseases are often disastrous, and have, in the past, received only amateur treatment by well intentioned soul-savers. But religious psychiatry, too, suffers from Freudian and other delusions and should itself be better psychoanalyzed. Strangers to religious experience themselves, when they can diagnose it correctly, are still inexperienced in healing such disorders. We shall begin our examination with the healthy aspects of religion and then refer the pathology to experts.

William James, who was a pioneer in this field, concentrated his analysis of varieties of religious experience on the relation between healthymindedness and sick souls. His sympathies were with the sick souls, and he scorned the healthy minded attitudes of Emerson and Christian Science by which he was surrounded. He had himself been a sick soul, and it is well worth while to study his own case. William James, after he had finished his medical studies at Harvard and had achieved the healthy mind of a scientist, continued his researches in Europe. While he was engaged with the scientific examination of the mechanisms that govern mind and emotion, he found himself going from one curative bath to another trying to get rid of melancholia and fits of depression. The baths were useless, and he finally decided that his faith in scientific determinism was causing the trouble: he wanted to believe in free will but could not. Finally, he resolved to force himself to believe in it "for one year." It is still not clear what cured him, but the experience of being a sick soul made a permanent impression on his psychology. He wondered why so many healthy minds became sick souls. And he was inclined to believe that the sick-soul experience was a healthy trouble for a good mind to get into. He discovered that the needs of sick souls were emotional rather than intellectual. In science, "believing *that*" or "doubting *that*" are related to having opinions more or less well founded; such opinions could be regarded as hypotheses to be tested by further evidence. But believing *in* and despairing *of* are attitudes of confidence and distrust that are thoroughly practical and emotional in their nature and consequences. Both the entertaining of hypotheses in the realm of opinion and the loss of trust in matters of fidelity are problematic experiences, calling for very different treatments.

In the life of devotion, when circumstances challenge a person's trust or fidelity, religious experience becomes self-conscious and seeks assurance, comfort, security. It is then that the confession of faith becomes a significant experience. To confess a faith does not mean to be certain; it means that one is aware that trusting goes beyond knowing. A confessed or self-conscious faith does not mean: This I believe to be true; it means: This I trust and I need to learn its reliability. A healthy mind sooner or later learns that faith and doubt go together, and that the justification of a faith is different from the verification of opinion. The discovery of this general human predicament is one of the fruits of experience and one of the grounds of intelligent religion. The discovery that living religiously is not living complacently or comfortably should be disconcerting, especially to a young mind. The constant tension between seeking and finding security, comfort, peace is central in mature religious experience. This tension may well lead to sickness at heart, but normally it is not a sickness unto death.

Creeds and Faiths

This psychological insight throws light on the relation between a public confession of religious faith and the attempt to
sum up one's own beliefs. A formal, public confession of faith
is a collective symbol and was once so termed. It is neither a
personal summary of personal opinions nor a collective declaration of common opinions of the members of a communion. "I
believe *in*" which begins a creed does not mean, "We all believe
this," though verbally it means precisely that. The formal confession of *the* faith is an act of devotion to the communion or
institution and to what it stands for. But this what-it-stands-for
or believes in, if it were really spelled out in historic detail,
could never be given a fixed and adequate definition. Its de-
clared creed arose in a time of confusion and doubt; it was a
declaration of the church militant faced with disintegration. At
that time it represented what the leaders of the faith could
agree on. But since it is primarily a symbol and confession of
historic continuity, it would be self-defeating to change it continually in order to keep pace with the changing beliefs of generation after generation. The creed is a mixture of history,
tradition, myth, experience, and fidelity—a kind of composite
portrait of the individuality of a particular communion. The
symbol is not, and never was a set of propositions to which the
members all subscribe. Any one of its propositions, taken out of
context, and interpreted by a member as his opinion, would
raise a group of issues that have had a long history and are still
confused. For example: "I believe a Holy Catholic Church"
does not mean: "We believe our church to be the Holy Catholic
Church," nor "We think that our church ought to be a Holy
Catholic Church," nor "There is a Holy Catholic Church." It is
supposed to mean, according to long-standing instructions: "We
trust in the invisible, unorganized, union of all whom Christ
has redeemed, who constitute the spiritual body of the faithful
under Christ their Lord." So interpreted, the belief is very generally held by all the saints, but this unanimity is exceptional.
Another declaration is much less precise: "I believe in the Res-

urrection of the body." Originally this was confessed to distinguish the particular Christian doctrine from the pagan belief in the immortality of the soul. A Christian is supposed to have some idea of the importance of the doctrine of the Resurrection. But there is no general agreement on precisely what it ought to mean. Though it is linked to "on the Third day," which is also in the Creed, there might be few who would take this literally. Many would be content with: "The life of the Church is the spiritual body (in the flesh) of the Risen Christ." These are now largely matters of doctrine, rather than of dogma, and are regarded as theological problems about which there are bound to be differences of judgment. In short, the corporate symbol of the Faith is a concise history of the loyalty of the members to the communion, but it has never been a unanimous set of beliefs.

The Plurality of Faiths

The psychology of confession of faith is related to the problem of the attitudes of religions toward each other. A proposition that it is the True Faith implies the falsity of those who deny it. Genuine fidelity has no such implications. In some languages there is no clear distinction between the truth of a proposition and the genuineness of an act of faith, nor between authority in matters of knowledge and integrity in matters of character. An error of judgment about matters of fact is an error, whether made sincerely or carelessly, whereas an act of infidelity is an act of carelessness. A proposition can be verified; an act or attitude must be justified. There is an ancient saying that the devil knows God but does not believe in him. The proposition that *God is* is not necessarily a religious belief; belief *in* God is a very different matter. To profess a god in whom one does not believe would be religious hypocrisy, but might be intellectual sincerity.

Accordingly, religions are more or less good or bad, but none is true or false. It is possible to tell the truth in many languages, but usually only one language is practical for one person, and no person is competent to tell the whole truth in any language. Similarly, there may be many good, serious, honest religions each devoted to its holy beings and sacred rites, without implying that only one of these can be the true religion. It is possible to be genuinely devoted according to a particular faith, without believing that those devoted to another faith must be wrong. There is no point in saying that all religions are equal. Their differences are real and important, but their respect or disrespect for each other should be based on specific differences and not on the general assumption that only one can be right or true or genuine.

The history of religions is full of holy wars, cruelty, tortures, persecution, martyrdom, and all kinds of bitter conflict. Gradually the competing faiths have given up world conquest. And so long as there are many languages, cultures, and traditions it is folly to expect a single religion. As the contacts, peaceful or hostile, between religions have increased, the possibilities for reciprocal understanding and respect have also increased. There has been for some time a general toleration and coexistence, but what is needed now, and is possible, is a genuine reciprocity of respect, and willingness to differ without conflict. The Buddhists have, on the whole, had the most peaceful record. As early as the third century B.C. King Aśoka, under Buddhist influence, proclaimed throughout his domain in India his famous edict:

> Concourse alone is best, that is, all should hearken willingly to the doctrines professed by others.

Nevertheless, Buddhists have been outspoken in making clear how they differ from others, and how different Buddhists differ from each other. They also state frankly what they regard as superstitions in other religions. But they are decent in their behavior toward those with whom they differ. Tibetan Buddhists have appropriated local Guardian Deities. Japanese Buddhists frequently honor Shinto gods at their Buddhist shrines. A prominent Japanese Buddhist recently explained to Christians:

In the Enlightenment experience there is no "God", no "creator" who gives commands, no "ego-soul", no "crucifixion", no "resurrection", no dichotomous distinction of good and evil, of friends and foes, no "judgment" to give, no paradise to lose, no immortality to obtain, no "savior" to accept, and no "kingdom" to enter.

(Daisetz T. Suzuki: *Buddhism and other Religions*)

But all this was a goodnatured explanation to those who had described Zen Buddhism as cultivating the Void.

Christian churches in the Orient find it difficult to sanction belonging to more than one religion, though the Oriental devotions often overlap and exclusive loyalty is not required. But Christians are seriously promoting ecumenical good will among religions. There are many religious leaders in the Orient and in the Occident who are urging more than tolerance among religions. A Christian lay leader in India, a prominent judge, made a frank and striking declaration recently:

Apart from the Sermon on the Mount and a few sayings of the Lord, we cannot get any guidance for our social and political problems from reading the Bible. We cannot by imitating Jesus get the necessary enlightenment for the problems of our day. God does not speak to us as he did in the days of the prophet. We have no ready access to him and he does not answer our questions. . . . If we take the "revelation" in different religions, we have to confess that they do not piece together to form an intelligible whole. . . . Every religion is a circle complete and perfect in itself. Though not consciously, yet in effect they start with a quest which they more or less achieve. Religions are really incomparable. . . . The idea that a person should be either a Hindu or a Christian should also be relinquished. . . . In India we must be prepared to see the infusion of Hinduism by Christian ideals and above all Christian life.

(Padipeddi Chenchiah, *Christianity and Non-Christian Faiths*

Such illustrations may suggest that there is a general interaction among religions today, criticizing each other, but at the same time learning from each other. The mere recognition that there are living faiths of mankind is a great gain, for this insight admits that religions are man-made and varied.

Types of Religious Experience

The variety of religions complicates religious experience in any one religion, for religions enrich each other. Though this interaction has been enormously enhanced by revolutionary means of communication and transportation, even the ancient history of the great religions shows extensive borrowings. There are enough foreign elements in all religions to provide in each a wide variety of religious experience. For example, during the so-called Hellenistic period, the centuries immediately B.C. and A.D., which was a period much like ours when Western and Eastern cultures met and their peoples were mingled, Greek, Roman, and Asian cults influenced each other and stimulated the growth of new religions.

In China and Japan there has been less separation than in Greece and Rome between the rites of civic or folk religion and the arts of meditation. Philosophical reflection and religious devotions are not separated, so that the line drawn between them in the West is quite arbitrary in the Orient. Confucianism, Taoism, Brahmanism, Vedanta, and Buddhism are all schools of sages as well as religious groups. The scriptures and traditions are those of sages, and their revelations are said to come from within rather than from above.

Despite these cultural differences there are a few types of religious experience that are quite general and that have noted examples in many religions. Three of these are:

1. *Mysticism.* Classical mysticism in the Western traditions was usually the experience of individuals in solitude, whereas in the Orient mystic experience is both common and social. In India, the art of meditation and disciplines (systematized by schools of *yoga*) is intended to cause the individual to lose his sense of self and to merge his individuality with the "ocean of being," or with a chosen divine being; thought gives way to unconsciousness as the mind is dissolved into union with the One. Some of the Western mystics adopted this same ultimate aim of absorption into the One, but carried on their meditations in a more dialectical and intellectual way. The Christian mystics

converted their prayers into various types of communion and ineffable union. The intense rapture of the Western mystics is quite different from the self-emptying, emotionless techniques of the Orientals. Institutional meditation is a prevalent type of devotion in the Orient.

2. *Pietism.* This is an emotional adoration of a divine Lord or Law or both. The theory of this type of experience is that love is perfected by having a perfect object. The Lord of Contemplation is a perfect being, and usually the perfection is conceived in human as well as divine attributes. Such love is the transformation of a natural affection into a holy, purified, dispassionate enjoyment, a kind of love resembling the disinterested, general love and providence of the Divine. Such piety is interpreted as a state of enlightenment by an inner holy spirit. This is quite different from both revelation and mysticism; it is a personal intimacy with a Lord or God and a reception of divine Grace.

Such pietism was experienced and expressed by Augustine and was cultivated in many Augustinian monasteries. From the eleventh century on there were fanatic forms of enthusiasm (seizure by an immanent spirit) and in the Renaissance such illuminism was opposed as pathological. The Molinists in Spain and the Jansenists in northern Europe created pietist circles and quietism, and the movement became widespread in the seventeenth and eighteenth centuries. The *devotio moderna* of the Friends of God was one of the chief centers of pietism, and *The Imitation of Christ* was one of the best-known works of devotional literature of this type. The movement took on both Catholic and Protestant forms and led to the formation of the Evangelical Churches among the Protestants and to devotions like *Corpus Christi,* The Sacred Heart of Jesus, and The Sacred Heart of the Blessed Virgin among Catholics. It led also to the Moravians, the Quakers, the Perfectionists, the New Lights, and the Great Awakening.

In Judaism the pietist movement is known as Chassidism. It spread from Eastern Europe during the seventeenth century and is still strong. In India it is known as *bhakti,* and its most influential literature is the *Bhagavadgita* and the hymns of Saint Singers of South India. In China and Japan this kind of experience is most evident in Pure Land Buddhism. In Islam it was practiced by the *sufis,* who still have communities.

3. *Ecstasy.* This experience of exaltation and inspiration may take the form of swoons or trances, or extreme quiescence. It is also the source of certain kinds of prophecy and oracles. In India, the state of *samādhi* (analogous to the Buddhist *nirvana*) is the culmination of the *yoga* discipline and meditation, and is defined as the release from all the fetters. Ecstasy is an aspect of some types of mysticism, but is not confined to mystic experience. It may be either a negative or a positive release.

Prophecy is another type, but less general among the religions than the three types listed above. It is important to note, however, that any kind of experience can receive a religious form of expression. Religious experience is not a unique kind of experience. Religious devotions are normally related to the types described, but are by no means confined to them. Religious media, too, are of all kinds: dancing, fasting, chanting, drunkenness, drugs, hypnotism, persuasion, and the rest—they all are found in religious forms somewhere. Religion may be civilized or wild, fine or folk, art or habit, good or bad, genuine or hypocritical.

XIII. Two Commandments

THE danger in a monotheistic, highly integrated devotion to God Universal is the danger of fanaticism. Of course, idolatry may be fanatical too, but it is more apt to be merely superstition. An enlightened monotheism has the problem of preventing wholehearted devotion from becoming an unreasonable, unhealthy obsession. Devotion is not necessarily a good or a virtue, and a highly integrated devotion, which takes a condescending attitude toward the many lesser responsibilities and goods, may become a terrible malady. A conflict between intense piety and the demands of daily social life can ruin both morals and religion. Even in normal experience, a high degree of devotion may be in constant tension with other important matters when they prove to be distracting.

The great monotheistic religions, therefore, have confessed their common and basic obligation to obey two divine commandments. They are aware that obeying both commandments is not a simple matter, for the two do not automatically go together. It is therefore very important for anyone who seeks to understand what genuine religion means in the face of these dangers to examine carefully how the two commandments cope with these dangers.

The traditional wording of these commandments varies somewhat as they are translated from one language into another, but an approximately standard version reads as follows:

> Thou shalt love The Lord, thy God, with a complete devotion of all that is in thee. This comes first and is thy greatest obligation. But there is another that is as essential as the first: Thy neighbor thou shalt love as a being like thyself. On these two loves hang the whole Law and all the Prophets.

There are serious difficulties in making either a general interpretation or a particular application of these commandments.

"Thou shalt love." If it is love that is commanded, the commandments are futile. Love comes from within, not on order. No parent, no lover, no authority can get results by demanding love. If I have not love, all commanding to love is hollow brass and verbal cymbals. The Almighty would be as helpless as a tough sergeant were he to shout such commands. Love and trust do not come on demand; they grow when nurtured and given proper ground. If it is love that He expects to receive, the voice of the Lord, when it speaks with genuine authority, cannot be the voice of an unconditional commander-in-chief. This must be the voice of One who takes the relationship of love for granted and who can speak to men in the context of love. Love must be the context of these commandments, but it cannot be the object that is commanded. The Voice then is not merely that of a Commander but of One Who demands that two kinds of love be distinguished: love to God and love to neighbor. The first point of the divine commandment, then, is that we understand the implication of a particular kind of love, namely, the love of "The Lord."

What makes this commandment a basic and serious obligation is that the Lord is not a god. To have a god is an ordinary and primitive trait in human experience, and scarcely needs to be commanded. As a rule, a god is provided by a culture, so that no individual should call a god "my god" in an exclusive sense. To appropriate such a god would be a conceit, to say the least. Gods are public by their nature. Hence, the reference in the commandment to "thy God" has a special significance, and implies more than a god of folk religion. Such gods are not loved; they are praised, feared, appeased, served, given tribute and sacrifices. In this commandment, which has a monotheist context, "thy God" is very different from having *a god.* "Thy God" is thine not as a property, but as something appropriated through devotion, through unconditional love; not a love that makes Him exclusively thine. He is appropriated personally in so far as in Him your personal devotion finds satisfaction.

It is customary to represent this kind of devotion as service to God. Moralists delight in preaching servitude to a divine master. And mystics, too, give themselves to God in an act of complete surrender. They become as nothing in the sight of God. Against such theories of self-enslavement this commandment says: Do not regard yourself as God's servant; give yourself in love to your God without giving yourself away. In other words, being religiously devoted or consecrated must be understood in its own terms. The encounter with God does not imply an external relationship, nor a social relationship, nor a subjection to authority. Nor is God adored as a "friend" or a "being like thyself."

Serving one's God is different from having a human lord. Lords, in the full sense of the word, are now rare; they have disappeared with feudalism and slavery. Though modern relations between employer and employee are still treated legally under the antiquated captions of master-servant law, there are few persons who know what it means to have a lord. In view of these cultural changes, lordship must be interpreted metaphorically. Having a lord implies a devotion that is dutiful and in service. It does not imply reciprocity or mutuality. If a lord makes friends of his servants, that is more than the relation generally implies. In short, love toward a lord, as distinguished from love among equals, is a willing, glad service, with possibly an element of friendship added, but not implied.

But now comes the difficult question: Who is THE Lord whom I make my God? THE Lord is clearly not a lord; there is none like Him. He is the universal master of a devoted life. Being devoted to THE Lord implies a kind of authenticity as well as integrity of devotion. Such devotedness of life may be expressed by formal devoutness or piety in a particular religion. But the sacraments of a church and divine service may also confuse or obscure the essential meaning of a particular life of general devotion. To one person The Lord may mean primarily The Truth; to another The Way; to another, The Light; to another the soul's peace that passes understanding. These are all metaphors, but an abstract definition would be false, if not meaningless. Lovers of The Lord find Him in different ways. The central point of the commandment is not to love "a Lord," but to love as "thy God" "The Lord," and this kind of love is a special kind of wholehearted devotion.

There are many causes and many persons and many institutions to which men and women are completely devoted. A man and a woman may be completely devoted to each other. Many a man may be blindly devoted to his work, profession, art, family, or country. In themselves such devotions are neither blind nor unnatural. They may be all-absorbing, completely integrating, without being fanatical, blind, or obsessive. But they are in danger of becoming so. A genuine sacred love of The Lord must be such a complete devotion without being blind or unenlightened. What this power may be which is unconditionally authoritative in a life without being unenlightened cannot be described in general terms. No one knows the essence of The Lord.

Nevertheless, it means something specifically to give all that one is or has to a Universal Lord. This religious devotion gives a more than personal dimension to a life, and involves it in a work, cause, communion that is general, transpersonal. Love of "The Lord, thy God" leads you into a community of devotion to a common good. Your God is also The Lord of a communion of persons devoted to The Lord. Communities of such communion may extend over many generations past and future. The more general the scope and meaning of such a community of devotion becomes, the more real or enlightening becomes the meaning of The Lord. This kind of love may be conceived in secular terms, but when it becomes religious, it is a very genuine religion.

To a person so completely committed to the love of The Lord, the Second Commandment comes with a sharp warning, and might well be introduced with a—"BUT"—"Thou shalt love thy neighbor!" The neighbor should be loved differently from The Lord. He is a being like yourself. He, too, may love The Lord as his God, or he may not. In any case, you must respect him as an equal, regardless of his religious devotion. Neighbors must be members in a secular community of self-respecting persons. Such neighborliness can be commanded as an obligation; it is not like friendship. And your devotion to The Lord must not violate this neighborly obligation. Neighborliness is a necessary virtue, not a voluntary love. I need to be reminded that my neighbor is a being like me. I need not respect my neighbor's morals, tastes, politics or philosophy, but these and mine must not prevent our neighborliness nor our religious devotions. If my neighbor is not my friend, not even God can command me to love him as a friend. Friendliness is not an obligation, but civil decency is. Those who love The Lord owe it to Him as well as to neighbors to be neighborly; religious devotion is no excuse for neglecting neighborliness.

In theory it is important to keep these two commandments apart, for they are radically different. In practice, of course, they may be considerably mixed. But the mixture is not good. If I find supreme, holy satisfaction in looking upon my neighbor as if devotion to his welfare were an aspect of my devotion to The Lord, my neighbor may resent my assuming that he needs my devotion. One who makes his moral obligations to neighbors merely a matter of obedience to a divine commandment is not being genuinely neighborly. In short, though moral obligations are also sacred, they should be understood as social.

It is by this time not only "all the Law and the Prophets" that "hang" or depend on an awareness and observance of these two commandments; any personality structure that is well ordered is based on them. Rather than use the metaphor of hanging or depending from on high, I would prefer to say that these commandments form the *terra firma* for both genuine religion and just society.

The Second Commandment means: **keep your religion civilized.**

XIV. Three Wise Men

In the Far East there lived three unemployed kings, whose meditations led them to conclude that they were too far from the West. One was a Taoist from Taiwan, one was a Buddhist from Tibet, and the third was a Parsee from Bombay. The more they discussed their own situations and that of the world, the more they became convinced that they should travel westward. They loaded their camels and caravans and started out over the great overland trade route. During the heat of the days, they camped at whatever market towns offered them hospitality, and rode during the nights, guided by their western star.

Their discussions about the future frequently touched upon the Western Paradise or Pure Land. None of the three expected to reach it, but their curiosity about it increased as they proceeded and they gradually became inspired by the idea that if they went far enough they might hear more reliable news about the nature and location of this Western Paradise than was available in the Far East.

It was King Taoist who claimed to know the way best and offered to guide the other two. He had learned from the ancient Chinese books of wisdom to distinguish the true way from misleading ways. The Tao, the natural way, could be felt once one were on it, but to get onto it was difficult and required training. He recited from Lao Tse's *Tao Te Ching:*

> The way we are going is not the real way; the truth I tell is not the real truth; and the map we are following is not the real map.

This startling news alarmed his fellow-travellers.

"What do you mean? Are we to disregard our star? Are you teasing? Is this what you Chinese call wisdom?" King Taoist was accustomed to such first reactions to the doctrine.

"Nothing," he explained, "is clear at first or intelligible in itself. Only by participating in The Great Participation, the One-and-All, does anything mean anything. Our way will become clearer to us as we follow our star. Heaven above is clear, but its partner, the earth below, is known as the dark uncarved block. By following its heavenly partner the earth gains enlightenment slowly. Heaven and earth belong together, and by keeping company they become known to each other. But each must stay in its own proper way. Hear again the words of Lao Tse:

> When the gods are at-One, they are spiritual; and the valleys when they stay where they belong become fertile. When all things achieve The Great Union, all things live and grow. It is within the World-Way that they live and grow silently, complete, form-less, invisible, unchanging, united, eternal and ever revolving, the Mother-World. I do not know its name and call it simply The World-Way.

It is in this way that we are now participating without knowing how or why, but it is only because of It that our ways are worth going."

"These are dark sayings," complained King Parsee, "The Darkness we know, to be sure, but what shows the Way?"

King Taoist broadened his usual, complacent smile, and confessed: "I can explain only by telling stories or reciting poems."

"Very well, continue," said King Buddhist, "For now we at least know that the explanations you give are not the real explanation."

"But listen carefully. A short while ago I was dreaming that I was a butterfly flitting here and there, not bouncing on a camel. For a moment, as I was awaking, I did not know whether I was a butterfly or on a camel, or even a flitting king. The dream was as genuine as the camel. All were real while they participated, the dreaming, the flying, the riding, the camel, so long as each went its own way. Then, for a moment, all became unreal, confused, as they got in each others' way. How they all fit together in the Way of the World, no sage can explain. In this way all things exist, but the whole story cannot be told."

There was a long silence. Finally King Taoist asked: "Shall I continue?"

"Is there more to say?" asked King Buddhist.

"There is this to be added from the Book of Wisdom," said King Taoist, 'We are accustomed to think that we have our beginning as individuals and that in the end we sink into the earth. But our real beginning is in the union of Heaven and Earth, The Great Origin, from which we slowly emerge as many individuals. Really we remain many in the One, held together mysteriously in The Great Sympathy that creates all differences. The love that unites us does not come from us; it embraces us. We enjoy our separate ways and loves only so long as we share in the universal World-Sympathy that holds all together. Our sympathies, our words, our ideas do not lead us onto the World-Way for they separate and differentiate. There is no reply to anyone who asks to be shown the Tao or who wants to know what it is. The reply would be more foolish than the question. The Way-of-the-World cannot be observed; it can only be followed—without effort, map, or guide. When the Way has been found, the going is effortless, spontaneous, like the ease of a fine artist. Only an expert can know such freedom of movement, and he can neither describe nor transmit it.' Reflect on this poem that comes to us from the eighth century:

> The wild geese fly across the long sky above.
> Their image is reflected on the still water below.
> The geese do not care to cast their images on the water.
> Nor does the water care to receive their images.

Hear also the words of Chuang Tzu:

> In the days of perfect nature men were quiet in their
> movements and serene in their looks. They lived together
> with the birds and beasts without distinction of kinds.
> There was no difference between the noble and the commoner.
> Being equally without knowledge, they had nothing to keep
> them apart. . . . They were upright and correct without knowing
> that to be so was the right way. They loved one another
> without knowing benevolence. . . . They helped without thought
> of virtue or reward. Hence they left no traces and we have
> no records of their affairs.

"I have often reflected on all this as I sat before the statue of The Goddess of The Great Sympathy, Kuan Yin, and of the innocent babe in her arms. I hope that somewhere in the West, too I shall find men who adore The Mother of the Great Sympathy and her innocent child. These human symbols have helped me to feel more concretely the silence, peace, and beauty of the Tao."

For a long time the spell of these words kept the three kings in silence as they jogged along. The starry heaven above revolving in quiet ease with the dark block below, dominated their imaginations and reflections. It was suddenly very real to them, this union of heaven and earth embracing the little way on which they were being carried, and the wonder of it all became almost overwhelming in the silence that followed upon the Taoist sermon.

It was several days before King Buddhist could decide why this Taoist Way-of-the-World was so different from the Middle Way discovered by the Lord Buddha. He concluded that the great universe of Heaven and Earth may have its own way, but that the human world and the cycle of birth and death is a smaller world, closer to human affairs and requiring a different Way. Finally he thought of the temple paintings in the Tibetan monasteries, which represented the world as in the jaws of the Demon of Desire. The world of human life and death is pictured as a great wheel, in which the lives of men and their endurance of misery are charted. To find a way of peace and repose in this kind of world is a very different problem from fitting into the union of Heaven and Earth. He decided to draw for his companions the picture of this wheel. With this before them they might appreciate Buddha's enlightened Way. He began:

"The wheel of birth and death is in the grip of a monster that symbolizes compulsive craving. In the hub of the wheel are its three chief forms: the serpent of anger, the pig of greed, and the bird of folly. The Buddha's Middle Way with its Noble Eightfold Path is intended to free men from the fetters of this demon and even from the whole cycle of birth and death. The wheel has six spokes, which frame six regions or states of man's existence in relation to these evils. The top segment is the Paradise of the Enlightenment. At the bottom are the hells of judgment and punishment. Adjacent to the hells, on the left, is the realm of animal existence; and on the right, the realm of hungry ghosts. Adjacent to Paradise in the upper half of the wheel is, on the left, the realm of human life; and on the right, the realm of demons. As the wheel rocks to and fro in the grip of Desire, the human spirit either rises or falls. Good eras alternate with bad ones. When the demons are rising toward Paradise, fleeing from hungry ghosts, mankind is falling towards animality and may sink lower into the hells of guilt and condemnation. When the demons are falling, men can rise toward Paradise by following the Buddhist Middle Way. If they succeed in obtaining true enlightenment and enter *Nirvana* or Paradise, they have escaped from all the perils of birth and death. If, on the contrary, men have fallen into a hell of anger, greed, or folly, they must regain human levels by a series of rebirths which carry them through the animal realm to human life and to another opportunity for escape from the rocking of the wheel. At present human life is in a degenerate era, when men are apt to fall into animality. During such an era (called *mappō*) men can be saved only with the saving grace or mercy of Amida Buddha, Lord of Paradise, and they must call on him to give them strength to follow the Middle Way. The coming Buddha, Maitreya, who will preside over the next, more fortunate era, will be the successor to the present Gautama Buddha, who enlightens the present era. Perhaps we shall hear news of the coming of Maitreya in the West, and of the beginning of a better world for mankind. Meanwhile the path to enlightenment is steep and difficult, for only Truth can set men really free. Let us hope that the Wheel of the Law will soon turn in our favor."

"Riding this rocking-wheel must be worse than riding a camel," suggested King Taoist. "It's a very strenuous life. And the chances of reaching Paradise seem to be worse than our chances on this road."

"It's a hard life, I admit," said King Buddhist, "but the Middle Way discovered by Lord Buddha is a true way, whereas the ways of extreme luxury or extreme asceticism that were lived before the Enlightenment were delusions."

During this whole Buddhist lecture King Parsee was attentive, but seemed irritated and uneasy. He appeared to be impatient to speak, and yet he kept quiet. After a bit of prodding by the two other kings, he finally burst out:

"Neither one of your ways seems to me very reasonable. The one is useless, and the other is hopeless. One relies too much on the harmony of Heaven and Earth; the other relies too much on a cold light to subdue the hot passions. It will not do to separate light and heat in this way. A good, practical way requires more energy, more reliance on fire. To me, fire is holy, divine; but it is also needed for real enlightenment. The reason I speak in this way about fire, is not primarily a matter of tradition. It is true that my traditions go back to the early sacrifices at the family hearth by our ancient ancestors. The domestic hearth and fire in the center of the courtyard was the place where sacred rites were performed and where the family fire was consecrated. But what is more important to me on this journey to the West with you is my belief that there is in the world a great conflict between two powers: the powers of Darkness and the powers of Light and Fire. I wish to learn more about this conflict because I believe it is going on in the West as much as in the East. We Parsees are confident that the Powers of Light and Enlightenment will conquer the Darkness, but we do not know how long the conflict may still endure."

Both the other kings showed an interest in knowing more about this conquest of evil and about how the conflict is being waged. They were not accustomed to think of the world as a battleground, and they hoped that the human conflicts that had been troubling the Far East were not made worse by even greater conflict in the West. King Parsee continued:

"All I can do is to tell you how our Prophet Zarathustra explained the conflict to us. The conflict in human nature between good and evil is part of a more general conflict in the world between two powers or types of energy—between firelight and dark destruction, between creative energy and violence. The constructive fire in the world creates light, life, and mind. Its counterforce of darkness destroys. Zarathustra taught us that fire sanctifies; it is a holy, life-giving power, the creative manifestation of the Holy Wise One, whom we call *Ahura Mazda* or *Ormazd*. He is the source of all good. But from the beginning of creation *Ahura Mazda* has been engaged in a struggle with the demonic power of darkness, *Angra Mainyu*. This struggle is not endless, for the great day of victory will come, when the Holy Wise One will lead his faithful followers onto the Bridge of the Separator, from which the children of Light will enter into the Eternal House of Song.

"I am a Parsee born into the family of the children of Light. We survive in exile from our native country and that of our Persian prophet, and in India we await the day of salvation when the Holy Redeemer, the Divine Righteousness, and the Divine Providence will free all of mankind from the power of darkness and evil. This will be the glorious and final enlightenment of the world. May it come soon."

Such exchanges of doctrine, wisdom, and faith gradually made of the three kings of Orient, whose acquaintance had been casual, genuine friends who understood each other both in their differences and in their common quest. They began to feel more intensely a common hope and expectation, and they convinced each other that the world was really ready for the great day of salvation and enlightenment. Soon they regarded each other as pilgrims, each meditating in his own way on their common quest. They even formulated a common prayer:

> Holy, holy, holy is the
> Dominion of the Lord of Peace
> Among men of good will who follow
> The Way, The Truth, and The Light.

The westward way of the three pilgrim kings was suddenly halted on the banks of a wide river, the Euphrates. They had crossed many a river, but this one was wider than the eye could see. Despair seized all three for they suspected that the Western Paradise was well guarded by deep, impassable waters so that it might be impossible to reach the West from the East. But a boat appeared on the horizon, and it was coming toward them. When it landed an old ferryman disembarked. Humbly greeting the royal travellers, he inquired their destination. The old sailor received their story with mixed amazement, excitement, and discouragement.

"I fear you still have a long and weary way ahead of you. I have ferried travellers in both directions, but the stories they have told me leave me ignorant. However, I venture a suggestion. If I understand you correctly, you are neither traders nor tourists, but royal seekers after wisdom in the West. Before you go too far west, you would do well to get the advice of experts. And if you are looking for peace as well as wisdom, you ought to be especially cautious going westward. Try to get some advance information, if you can. Now it happens that up the river there is a city where I am sure you could get the latest and best information about the subject of your interest. If, instead of crossing here, you go upstream along the east bank which takes you in a northwesterly direction, you will find a much easier crossing. And besides, the crossing will take you to Babel. This is an international headquarters for information and travel advice, a great metropolis where men live in proud skyscrapers, huddled together like bees in a hive. But unlike bees, the citizens are strangers to each other. They are composed of many nations and speak many languages. Consequently they understand each other only superficially. Nevertheless they enjoy their confusion at close quarters, and carry on all kinds of trades and crafts. They make and exchange anything, translate anything, transport to anywhere, and quarrel over the most trivial matters. Theirs is a highly developed civilization, the envy of the whole world. They have not only high apartments, but libraries, schools, museums, temples, shopping centers, lawyers, and police. You will certainly find there any religion for which you may be seeking, as well as sages, professors, executives, and specialists on any subject. Three wise men would not be much of a novelty there, but three royal pilgrims would cause quite a stir and you would get abundant publicity and a royal reception."

The three kings received this advice with the greatest thanks, amazement, and incredulity. They begged the ferryman for a bit of time for deliberation. On the following day they informed him that they wished to cross with him instead of deviating from their course. The course of their star was due west. Besides, they admitted, Babel would make them ill at ease, for they were not accustomed to such a wealth of services. After getting across the Euphrates, the kings had many miles and deserts to ride through before their way became Near East, then Nearer East, until they finally arrived at regions ruled by a Western Power.

At the King's palace in Jerusalem they began to feel the impact of the Roman Empire. Here they were received formally as visiting royalty, but when they explained the object of their pilgrimage, mentioning The Western Paradise and The Prince of Peace, they felt a chill come over the palace. The court circles and diplomats were immediately called into closed session and counterspies were appointed. The three kings received considerable information about places that they would do well to visit. And on leaving they were told, "Kindly report back to us, so that we can join you in veneration." Being both kings and wise men, they were soon aware that in Roman territory there reigned the same kind of insecurity that they had experienced in the Far East. The object of their quest was subversive.

Under these circumstances the three pilgrims decided to keep out of court circles and to inquire among the common folk about The Western Paradise and their other concerns. Here they found a very different moral climate. What was being dreaded in the palace as a day of doom, was being expected presently by the people as a day of deliverance and redemption. Prophets and shepherds, all were seeing visions and hearing angelic voices proclaim the good news. All were ready to welcome the Prince of Peace. The kings also heard of a New Jerusalem; but the Western Paradise?—It might be still further west!

They had not been long in Roman territory before their star took a sudden turn to the East. By this time the kings were neither shocked nor sorry that their westward way had ended. They gladly followed back east. We have been told nothing about the return journey, except that they went by a different way. They had become three different kings—and wiser men.